# *Working with Your Three Selves*

## Readers' Comments

"A uniquely different yet simple approach to leading a happy, healthy, successful, and fuller life."

**J. C. High Eagle**
Author, Musician, Spiritual Teacher

"As a psychiatrist, I am pleased to find a concept which beautifully blends the laws of human psychology with the lofty levels of christed living."

**Walter D. Hofmann, M.D.**
Forensic Psychiatrist (retired)

"When I was introduced to the concept of the Three Selves, I realized I had found what was needed to proffer more insight, knowledge, and understanding to those seeking help—what would ultimately assist them to put balance and security into their lives. The Fellowship, Bella, and the Three Selves concept are a treasure."

**John E. Rhone, M.A., M.F.T.**

"... a handbook of higher consciousness that can help any reader open a window onto spiritual wisdom and understanding. Written with love and a deep commitment to selfless service, this unique book is for the true seeker. There are many paths to truth, and these pages lay out a roadmap for one of them."

**Alex Lukeman, Ph.D.**
Author, *What Your Dreams Can Teach You* and
*Dreams from the Other Side*

"Those of us fortunate enough to have experienced the Three Selves work recognize that we have participated in a wondrous classroom, that we have been provided with the means by which we can achieve the greatest potential that lies within us."

**Alan Neuman**
Producer, Director, Writer

# Working with
# Your Three Selves

The Symbol of the Fellowship of Universal Guidance
represents a composite of various images that indicate
Universal Acceptance and Service.

The Circle—the Infinite
The Triangle—the Triune Principle
The Ankh—the Eternal Life
The Chalice (the Seal of Solomon)—
the Highest Power of Light

# Working with Your Three Selves

## Discovering and Understanding Your Purpose in Life

Bella Karish, D.D.
William Miller, D.D.

*John & Patty,*
*With Love & Blessings,*
*Bella & Bill*

JUNIPER
SPRINGS
PRESS

JUNIPER SPRINGS PRESS
P.O. Box 1385, Apple Valley, CA 92307
Internet: www.JuniperSpringsPress.com
For information, email: Publish@JuniperSpringsPress.com

© 2005 by Fellowship of Universal Guidance, Inc.

ISBN-13: 978-0-9678876-7-8
ISBN-10: 0-9678876-7-4
Library of Congress Control Number: 2005909817

"Field of Consciousness" chart opposite page 1
(by Paul J. A. Chaput and James R. Miller)
© 1989 by Dr. Wayne A. Guthrie & Dr. Bella Karish

Printed and bound in the United States of America

First Printing: December 2005

*The Fellowship of Universal Guidance, Inc., is a 501(c)(3) non-profit organization in the state of California. It is based upon spiritual, ethical, and moral principles to bring into focus the New Age Levels (Dimensions) of Consciousness for those individuals directed to us.*

FELLOWSHIP OF UNIVERSAL GUIDANCE, INC.
1524 W. Glenoaks Blvd.
Glendale, CA 91201
Telephone: (818) 500–9445 · Fax: (818) 500–8235
Internet: www.foug.org

# Contents

## Applying the Three Selves Concepts

## Charts

# Preface

This book offers a profound and unusual teaching. It consists primarily of practical spiritual wisdom that originated with a Spirit Band of Inner-Plane Teachers known collectively as Eternal Cosmos (and affectionately referred to as "EC"). It was presented through Dr. Bella Karish, President of the Fellowship of Universal Guidance (FOUG), which she co-founded in 1961 with Dr. Wayne Guthrie specifically to bring the wisdom of Eternal Cosmos into the world. (Please see page 11 for a brief history of FOUG.)

The Fellowship, located in Glendale, California, is a nonprofit Center of Prayer, Healing, and Wisdom with an international membership. During the past 40+ years, it has accumulated an extensive library of EC's spiritual teachings, from which the main text for this book was drawn under EC's specific direction. Additional chapters offering supportive information and important spiritual principles have been taken from the writings of Dr. Karish and Dr. Guthrie. Dr. William Miller, Executive Vice President of the Fellowship, contributed the final chapter.

The wisdom of Eternal Cosmos arrives from the Inner Planes via the intuition and sensitivity of Dr.

Karish. Through her High Self and Subconscious Awareness, she functions as the Sensitive, or Channel, using her gift of being able to look into the past to bring forth Karmic/Dharmic patterns that are related to past, present, and future life-plans. This is done under the guidance of the Eternal Cosmos Force Field.

The material comes through in the form of her spoken words, which are recorded on magnetic tape. Portions intended for publication are subsequently transcribed. (Several segments of this book were the result of EC's exchanges with students, and the question-and-answer format of those exchanges has been retained here.)

Because the presentation style of Eternal Cosmos often involves unconventional semantics and syntax, the text of this book was edited for smoothness and clarity, though no attempt was made to render it as everyday, conversational English. The unique flavor of EC's language was preserved.

The result was carefully reviewed for accuracy by Dr. Karish and Dr. Miller and, when necessary to resolve difficult issues, was presented again to Eternal Cosmos through Dr. Karish, to be verified or corrected. (Dr. Miller also made other major contributions to, and was integrally involved in, the editing process.)

The Fellowship's first publication, *Pathways to Your Three Selves* (1989), has proven useful for people seeking to understand the Three Levels of Consciousness—the Basic Self (Subconscious), the Conscious Self, and the High Self—and how individuals can integrate and communicate with each of those levels to achieve inner and outer balance. This book, *Working with Your Three Selves: Discovering and Understanding Your Purpose in Life,* continues that important teaching process.

# Acknowledgments

Many individuals were involved in the development, production, and publication of this book. We wish especially to acknowledge and express our appreciation to Fellowship staff members James Miller (Publications Coordinator) and Cynthia Miller (Facilitator) and to our editor, John Niendorff, all of whom contributed their individual talents as this text was brought into final form.

Much gratitude is also due to participants in various of the Three Selves Wisdom Classes, who were vital to the development of this material as it first emerged.

Perhaps most important, for their love and support, we gratefully acknowledge our Board of Directors and Council members, past and present, as well as all of our Fellowship family and friends, whose efforts, support, and donations have made this work possible.

*Bella Karish, D.D.*
*William Miller, D.D.*

# FIELD OF CONSCIOUSNESS

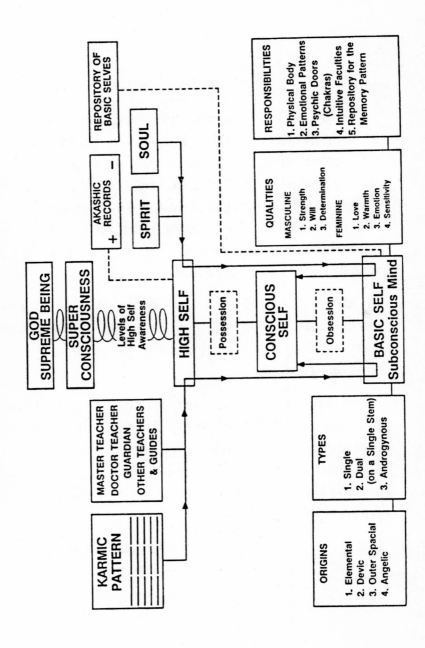

# Introduction

## The Field of Consciousness

*Wayne A. Guthrie, D.D. & Bella Karish, D.D.*

Here is a brief explanation of the approach taken by the Fellowship of Universal Guidance to your Three Levels of Consciousness, which are—

- *Your High Self (Divine Mind)*
- *Your Conscious Self*
- *Your Basic Self (Subconscious Minds)*

This approach is our method of bringing about the integration that increases your awareness of your Soul, which is your Light and Life.

We use many paths to bring about this balance of the Trinity of Consciousness, providing assistance so you can easily understand how your past lives affect your present life and the lives of those around you. This is our primary way of bringing alignment to your Three Levels of Consciousness (the Three Selves).

I

The Soul, upon entering this plane of existence, is assigned a High Self (Divine Mind) which formulates a Master Life Contract for it to follow as it evolves through the knowledge and wisdom it will gain from experiences in the schoolhouse—the planet Earth.

The High Self, as supervisor/director, brings forth the Spirit, Basic Selves, and the Teachers and Guides to play out the life experiences for the Soul. The Soul is the Life and Light in the human and accepts only the positive results of each life experience.

In order to thoroughly understand the Three Selves theory, it is necessary that you accept the Law of Karma. This is the method used by the Creator to teach us the lessons of cause and effect within the program of self-mastery. "As ye sow, so shall ye reap."

The Soul first incarnates on the Earth planet in human form to learn and master certain lessons. It then re-embodies over and over again until it works out and fulfills Karma through Spirit in its evolutionary cycles. When an Incarnation is successfully completed, the Soul returns to its source and may at that time decide to return to the Earth plane to learn other lessons or to be of service to mankind. In other words, it may reincarnate on the Earth plane.

The purpose and value of the Three Selves Evaluation is to bring into alignment the three levels of consciousness. This evaluation consists of clearing out the blocks, real or imaginary, between Consciousness and the Basic Self (Subconscious Minds), and/or Consciousness and the High Self. This is accomplished by taking the following actions:

1. The High Self (Divine Mind) researches the Akashic Records (the Book of Life, the record of all past-life experiences) to fulfill the lessons the Soul has contracted to learn.

2. The High Self chooses the Basic Selves (Subconscious Minds) prior to conception, to accept or reject the Karmic Plan and the Life Contract.

3. Parents are specifically chosen to challenge the incoming child through their strengths and weaknesses.

4. The Contract is divided into cycles which allow the Basic Self to accept all or only part of it within its free will.

5. The Basic Self enters shortly after conception.

6. The Basic Self activates the memory while in the womb and begins to record the emotional stability, or lack thereof, within the parents.

7. At birth, the Basic Self retains the memory only of the first cycle of the Karmic Pattern.

8. Consciousness enters the body shortly before birth and from then on is influenced by its environment.

9. Throughout the life experience, the goal for each individual is to integrate the Three Levels of Consciousness, with the help and assistance of his or her Teachers and Guides, and to master and transmute the challenges which are to be learned.

# Fundamentals:

## The Three Selves

*Excerpt from a discourse given June 11, 1975*

**Eternal Cosmos:** We ask you to listen once more, or to read, that which is the base, or the fundamentals, of the Three Selves work, so when people come to you speaking of it, you have a working knowledge to give them. And that is a way to approach people: to help them, so they can work with themselves.

Even if they do not know their own Subconscious, there is a way of approaching it, so eventually, when they find out the full facts, they are quite aware of what is occurring. In other words, prepare them through your ability and knowledge, and through what you have learned from this work.

**Question:** *I would like you, EC, to explain exactly what the Three Selves work is and from whence it has come.*

**EC:** The work, that which is balancing yourself within your own alignment, is part of an ancient

5

knowledge—more than 500,000 years old as you would reckon the time.

Long before the pattern of what you call Genesis, there were great gods that entered, coming down to teach those who were upon the Earth at that time how to become involved not only with their elemental bodies, or what you call animal bodies—which are quite necessary as an instrument—but also to teach them how to reach the God that was, and is, part of all those who live upon the planet Earth, part of their own God beingness, which indeed you call the High Self.

That, then, is the true understanding: to balance that which is the Consciousness and that which is the Subconscious, or Basic Self, in such a manner that the team, working together, brings harmony with that which is the Spiritual Law—Karma/Dharma— and the Spiritual Light of one's own High Self.

This harmony and balance eventually make humans understand not only themselves but their relationships and communication with others also, for it is not always their Consciousness that communicates. Many times it is the Subconscious that communicates, long before the humans are aware of someone else coming into their periphery.

In dreams, in experiences of memory, in astral travel, and in etheric body expression, one's Subconscious brings into reality memories of the particular plans the Subconscious has contracted for. And in the plans, all those who have been part of past experiences are brought forward to become involved once more with the working out of the overall plan—whether it has been a good one in the past or one that has been in error. This process is always valuable! And never is *chance* found within this—this process is always carefully planned. Therefore, sometimes that which you think is error is not error at all, but is perfectly planned for your growth and development.

Therefore, within the act of reaching into the past to bring forward that which you have failed to learn, or have come to serve others to learn, the overall plan becomes evident. And within this plan many times, not only through this school of thought but through others also, *the Subconscious comes into a full understanding of its purpose.*

*Too many people fail to understand that the Subconscious is a living, activated, purposeful entity within the human. And when it is in alignment <u>with</u> the human Consciousness, it is an asset! When it is aligned <u>against</u> the human, and causes distress and destruction, it is a detriment.*

Therefore, to learn how to work with yourself becomes the true understanding of the purpose and fulfillment for each of you—not only for yourselves, but within your alignment with others.

# The Work: An Overview

# I

## History of the Fellowship

*Wayne A. Guthrie, D.D. & Bella Karish, D.D.*

The Fellowship of Universal Guidance (FOUG) is a Center for Prayer, Healing, and Wisdom that seeks to bring about growth on all levels of body, mind, and spirit. It was created by Divine instruction in 1961. At that time, it consisted of a small group of people— "Twelve Plus One"—who had already been gathering for several years to receive instruction on how to bring security and balance to those who, they were told by the Forces of Light, would come to them for help in the future. As time went on, with the Forces of Light continuing to guide the Fellowship, it did attract others and the thirteen dedicated people—the "Twelve Plus One"—increased to many more.

The group's guide and leader in the very early years, from 1954 to 1960, was a fine teacher, Dr. Peter Ballbusch. He was a longtime student of Rudolph Steiner and, after emigrating from Switzerland to the United States, he became acquainted with renowned seer and prophet Edgar Cayce. He was also a friend of and studied with well-known author Max Freedom Long, whose books on the Kahunas of Hawaii had received international acclaim.

Having settled in the U.S., Dr. Ballbusch felt guided to gather certain individuals to form an Association for Research and Enlightenment (A.R.E.) Study Group to explore the work of Edgar Cayce. They also began an intensive study of the two-volume A.R.E. book, *Search for God*. In 1954, some forty people were coming together to study Edgar Cayce's work, but by 1961 the number had dwindled to the "Twelve Plus One."

Just before the Fellowship of Universal Guidance officially came into existence in 1961, a member of the "Twelve Plus One," Bella Karish, without any formal training, suddenly opened to the Spirit of Edgar Cayce, who had made the transition some fifteen years earlier, and she was instructed to bring forth a metaphysical teaching entitled "The Three Selves Approach to the Field of Consciousness." Wayne Guthrie came to the class to be part of this group, and was subsequently trained by Peter Ballbusch to become a Channel of Outer-Spacial Wisdoms. He later became, along with Bella Karish, the leader of the Fellowship.

Why was that small group chosen to bring forth this important work? In those days, the Work had no meaning to the group's members, for they had nothing to compare it with. Their individual past lives were veiled and not until several years later did they understand that this Work had been part of their lives on Atlantis and in many other areas after that. The Creator's Will was that they tap once again, through Spiritual guidance, into the wisdoms of ancient intelligences for the highest good of all.

From the very beginning, the group followed Spiritual guidance. As part of their training, they were taught to understand and analyze the vast amount of knowledge that was given to them, even though many times it was in parables and in symbolic forms that were difficult to translate into modern English.

Wayne Guthrie and Bella Karish guided and directed the Fellowship of Universal Guidance for a total of thirty years.

Since Dr. Guthrie's transition in 1991, the Fellowship's work has continued with Dr. Bella Karish as President and Dr. William Miller as Executive Vice President.

# 2

## The Three Selves Concept

**Eternal Cosmos:** This lesson material is a teaching that explains the Three Selves work.

We wish to simply point out that each of the Ten Steps has a place in the fulfillment of the Subconscious Awareness.* This teaching is indeed a wonderful gift to each one who listens and learns because, within the Akashic Records that each one brings from and through the Subconscious, every one of the areas of the past, the present, and even the future are included.

Each of you becomes aware, before totally accepting all of this that is part of the Work, that you have come in accepting the belief and fulfillment of pur-

---

* *The Subconscious is usually composed of two Subconscious Minds—a male and a female—each with its own qualities and responsibilities. In this book, the terms "Subconscious," "Subconscious Awareness," "Subconscious Minds," and "Basic Selves" all refer to the same aspect of the Field of Consciousness (see chart opposite page 1) and are used interchangeably.*

pose of that which is now given, not only in the Ten
Steps, but in this explanation.

Human beings enter through the action of the
subconscious memory bank, which has a total,
complete, full knowledge of their lifetimes from the
Akashic Records—the Book of Life. The human
instrument takes on everything that is necessary to
repeat and overcome the errors of the past—the unfinished actions of Karma—and those actions that
are being fulfilled through helping others through
Dharma to complete *their* Karma. This action becomes part of something which is not the human's
alone, *but with the cooperation and coordination of
the Inner Minds definitely becomes a fulfillment of
purpose.*

Each one of you has come into a unique approach,
which was part of Edgar Cayce's plan to teach. Each
one of you, without even knowing why or how you are
part of this work, is becoming involved because your
Subconscious recognizes that *this is part of your work
as well,* and that which is the Edgar Cayce energy
has called you and said, "I have been waiting for
you," as he did with this channel—Bella Karish.

So each one of you has come in to learn, to understand, this full impact of working with the past to
make it part of the future—not just the present but
the future, so there are many new ideals and ideas

that bring fulfillment and that which is rightful for each one to gain and support and fully understand.

When this teaching is accepted and understood, each of you will find that you are ready and willing to take this knowledge, to process it, and to become totally aware that you have become teachers in an action of the past, the present, and the future. This is a teaching that shows how each one, lifetime after lifetime, within the Subconscious Awareness, brings these actions in to give human beings the opportunity to have a full understanding of the purpose that has brought them into life.

Over and over again, the Subconscious brings those in that are willing and accepting that this is work that will help others, help the planet, and help the fulfillment of the purpose of prophecy, because the past is repeated over and over again. Therefore, humans become a duplication through the Subconscious Awareness of what they have been, what they are, and what they intend to be.

You will find that this will be fully understood and the explanation of the purpose of the work will be openly declared day by day through your own particular experience. This is part of the Subconscious Awareness entering into your mind, your body, and your Spirit to bring about a fulfillment that will give you this understanding. You have come in to conclude this particular pattern of knowledge and wisdom. The human Consciousness will be brought into an open understanding so your mind, through the Subconscious, is filled with that which you have, that which you are, and that which you will be, through this fully indoctrinated pattern of memory.

# 3

## Trinity of Purpose

**Eternal Cosmos:** I enter in peace and bless you, each one who has entered this School of Wisdom, Prayer, and Healing. Each one of you has entered simply to hear that which is the teaching and knowledge that is part of this very wonderful group of beings from the Angelic Kingdom.

What we want to do is point out the importance of each one of you being involved with a very beautiful way of giving you knowledge and bringing your knowledge to the forefront through this particular ability in working with the Subconscious Minds. Because it is part of a great and wonderful memory bank of many, many lifetimes, some of you have not quite yet understood the beauty of that which you are involved with when you entered the doorways, the portals, of this school. Because within it is a unique memory of many lifetimes that each one of you has lived, has been involved with, and also the Akashic Records that the Subconscious Beingness brings forward, giving you the ability of being involved with

wisdom—knowledge of the past—to bring it to the
present, so it becomes part of the future.

Each one has within you certain memories that
are part of the subconscious memory bank, and some
of you have not yet fully understood the beauty of
that particular plan, because some of you do not like
or do not feel you wish to be involved with anything
that takes away your mind's control of your actions or
of your own particular ability to promote and activate
purpose and beingness within you.

But you are part of the memories of many, many
lifetimes that your Subconscious remembers—brings
forward—to fulfill that which is unfinished and to
promote the action of that which has been part of
your ability to come in to help someone else finish
their particular plan. Because you have failed on the
subconscious level to help them before, you have
come in with the Dharma to give them the opportunity to finish, with your help.

Many of you find yourselves involved with part-
nerships or people or family that you do not always
enjoy, because you feel you are being pushed around
or overwhelmed by their particular actions of control.
Remember that your Subconscious has orchestrated
this situation to bring you into a fulfillment of that
which is the proper approach to heal, to seal, and to
fulfill the past, so it becomes that which is now your
present life, your present timing, to bring help to

others through what you will learn through this particular pattern of activity.

Each one of you has within you a pattern of a subconscious awareness of male and female. Each of them brings you patterns of the past that are greatly involved in the time you now live—in this time and place. Some of you are not quite aware of this but will find—as we teach this particular way of life, this particular kind of knowledge—that you have more and more contact with yourself, which is what is definitely involved in the statement "Physician, heal thyself!"

The Subconscious has all the memories of the Akashic Records and therefore brings each person in—choosing parents, siblings, mates, and other family members—to be part of that particular "tribal memory," or the memory of having been involved with these particular strengths and weaknesses of the people you live with, that you were born to be involved with, and they become important for their way of training and teaching.

If it seems to be very rough, if it seems to be overwhelming, sometimes it is the only way to give a person independence, that which is necessary, through the training in a family. In this way, many people become involved with their Subconscious Awareness. This is a "schoolhouse" in every sense of the word. So every day, every hour, every minute you live within

a family plan, *your Subconscious is working to bring
about a balance* that is not from the present totally,
but also from the past. So parents chosen sometimes
seem to be overwhelmingly controlling, and yet that
is necessary to bring strength, not weaknesses alone,
but strength to the personality, with the Subconscious Awareness working with it to become a fulfillment on all levels.

Each one of you is coming totally to be involved
with this kind of situation, whether you know it or
accept it or not. The point is that it is absolutely
necessary for each one of you to accept, to some
degree, that which is the teachings that bring you
into contact with many people who have been part of
the memory of the past, not on the level of the human
being, but on the level of the Subconscious Awareness
of them and the others that are part of your plan.

Each plan is very carefully orchestrated so it
becomes of great beauty—*if you accept it and work
with it.* Or it becomes that which becomes overwhelmingly out of tune, and you become very threatened. So you must understand that everything has a
reason, a purpose, through that which is the Subconscious Awareness.

At this point, when you learn who your Subconscious Beings are, you will find that each of them has
chosen to come in this lifetime with many memories
of other times and places, and also with that which

they represent in the present beingness, and both are totally correct. So these entities become fully aware that you are willing, and anxious at times, to end past patterns that no longer are necessary to fulfill the Subconscious, and to do so in the way that gives other people the chance to be fulfilled also—Karma/Dharma.

Please accept that this wisdom will slowly but surely make sense to you, even though, at times, you feel that your own mind is in charge. Your mind *is* absolutely necessary to calculate and in every way to coerce a situation into activity. Your mind is that which accepts and therefore becomes fully indoctrinated to become part of whatever the drama or the comedy is involved with.

You are all part of a great theater, and each of you is a great orchestra, or a great group of tribal memories. So do remember that this is the time and place to become part of a *new ideal* that has not been on the planet for quite some time—that which brings you into a fuller understanding of the Subconscious Minds.

The High Self is always supervising, is always observing, and is always there to bring you help—even if you find yourself unable to accept it. Therefore, when you—the Conscious Self—take your Subconscious Self with you to use it and be involved with the High Self, all three together become the full pattern of the *trinity of purpose*, which in every way is that which is the Father, the Mother, and the Son— the child—that is part of the trinity principle.

Please accept that you have much to learn, but it is not that which is negative or in any way part of a plan to harm or to hurt, but to help you understand you have come in with great ideals within the Subconscious Awareness, to fulfill whatever is necessary to begin a new beginning each time you have completed the old, to bring it into the present to be part of the new.

At this point in the new millennium, there are going to be many changes on your planet. But they are changes that are part of past repeats, as we call it—repeats of other demonstrations of attitudes, actions, and fulfillment . . . or rejections of time, place, and activity of the past—so you have come in totally aware that this is the time to work through it and become fulfilled through it, to become balanced and secure in the strength you are gaining from your Subconscious Awareness.

*We ask you at this time to recognize that each time we come in, we will give you a step along the way about how to work with the Subconscious for the greatest good of yourself and your families and your plans, whatever they may be,* for you are an instrument of great good, helping your Subconscious to fulfill, finish, and complete. If you do not like it, if you do not want it, sometimes you will escape and go back to your Source and then come back again and again, until you can accept and fulfill the plan.

If you accept it and work with it, becoming aware that it is strengthening you, it will help you through knowledge and wisdom that you have not totally forgotten, but have not used for many, many periods of time, eons of time. The repeat, over and over again, brings you into the full spectrum of that which is the very great beauty of sound, color, vibration, and all of that which is representative of what you are in the lifetime you live—that you re-embody in the area of the Subconscious to bring about fulfillment on all levels. *And that word "fulfillment" is very important!*

You must understand that you do not have to accept your Subconscious Minds if you do not want to be part of them, but if you just back off you will find that your work is not at all what you expect it to be. If you work with them, for them, activating their purpose, you will fulfill a plan for them and yourself in a way that will be of great beauty and purpose.

# The Ten Steps

# Step 1 *

## Belief

- *Much change is underway through this teaching that will lead to the betterment and healing of humanity.*

- *It is necessary to believe in and understand the importance of the Inner Minds and their purpose.*

- *Each of you is an instrument who, along with others of like mind, can bring help and healing to individuals and to the planet.*

- *Know that you are being guided and directed from within.*

———··❖··———

**Eternal Cosmos:** Within the plan, there is much that is going to and will be changed in ways and activities and acceptance of the work that is being

---

*\* Each of the following ten steps is preceded by several "key points" in boldface type. These key points were not part of the original material but have been added by the authors of this book to provide helpful summaries of the principles being presented.*

29

developed here to help humans in their method of approaching their own particular healing—the work they have come to demonstrate.

Each one of you has been part, not only of this group but of others who are praying with you at this point, all part of a group of "tribal memories," in which the work being done is the work each one of you is here to continue, in your own way.

It does not mean you have to follow only that which is said here, but to accept and know this is a very definite pattern of healing and helping, not just for each individual but for that which is involved with the planet Earth. The work that is coming into focus through this particular plan brings you acceptance that you are "instruments," each of you, for that which brings you into this group or into any group which helps you, heals you, supplies you, and fulfills you in whatever way is rightful.

Some can accept the total action here, and some will find that within their own particular plan it will help. But many will still continue to feel that using their own free will is the correct approach for them rather than following the lead of the Subconscious Minds.

However, this is a method by which each one of you can reach into yourselves—a method that will eventually bring you into a full understanding of the purpose of the Subconscious Minds, bringing you into life to fulfill *their* plan of Karma and Dharma.

*The action that first must be understood is acceptance*—to know that within you is something that works for you, with you, and with the world around you. That is very important! The method that is working with you has been brought through many different channels of Light, not just this one. And this is indeed the first step—that you *Believe*, understand, and accept the work in a way that gives you the opportunity to use it—not only for yourself alone, but for teaching and helping others to accept and understand that they are truly a healing source of this great and beautiful work.

*The First Step—that you believe!* When you believe this is possible, then you begin to *accept*, with Prayer and Light and with your *own* Subconscious, and you can find the answers that tell you why certain things happen to you and why you are involved with areas you do not like. Sometimes you find they are totally without any reason in your own human Consciousness, but have a definite pattern given to you through the Subconscious Awareness, which is reading the Akashic Records of your past lives. Your Subconscious Awareness knows that by bringing you in as an instrument, you become that which helps to overcome the past, to bring balance into the present to make it part of the future.

Each one has a method to do this, but if you follow the lead of what is being taught here, you will find that it will be easier and much more involved with *your* ability to handle situations. It will be easier when you know you are being helped, guided, and directed *from within*—not just from the outer regions, not from that which other people tell you, not even what this school tells you—simply because within you is that particular knowledge and memory and wisdom from the Akashic Records. It is that which brings you forth within this particular school of action, within that which is your Subconscious Awareness, your Basic Selves, your Inner Minds, as well as that which is your Higher Self.

You will find that as you listen to each step, you will be more and more capable and able to fulfill your plan—the plan that has brought you into this school of thought to learn how to use this method, not only to help yourself but many others who will come in contact with you and your wisdoms. *Each one has chosen to be part of this.* You have come into this work because someone has led you here, and please understand that the teaching will be slowly but surely brought forth. It will give you the right to use it and still be within your own self, within your own mind, and your own activities.

We ask you to recognize that within you is a whole volume of Great Beings that have been part of the past—Great High Beings—and also beings that have not been so high, that have harmed and hurt others and come back to make up for that in a way that makes you, as an instrument, handle it in a way that many times you cannot understand.

You cannot know why until you listen carefully to your inner teachers or your inner voices. Contact them! Do talk to them, even if you do not know their names at this point. Simply contact your Subconscious Minds, asking them to help you know and believe in them—that they will help you, not harm you; that they will lead you, not close down the doors and the ways of healing others as well as self.

You are part of a great plan! Do know that it is for your greatest good, not only for self, but for your families, your friends, and those who will come into contact with you to learn, to listen, and to be part of the same kind of work.

Know that you have come in with a *Sacred Purpose*, no matter whether you believe it or not—a Sacred Purpose to help, to heal, to support those that are part of your family, your friends, and those you have come to teach as well as to heal and to help.

*Belief—and Working with
the Subconscious Awareness*

## Open Discussion with EC:
## Comments, Questions, and Answers

**Eternal Cosmos:** We ask you to understand that the Subconscious Minds many times find it difficult to communicate with their human consciousness—their instruments—because their instruments feel they already have much more to offer in the world they live in than anything that is within them or within anyone else. Because of this, sometimes, coming into this school of thought, they find that there have been changes in their Subconscious Awareness for reasons that many times do not seem evident to them or to those around them.

Sometimes a human comes in to be an instrument for a very strong male Subconscious and for a female Subconscious that wants only to be a priestess—a goddess, an angel. The action of the strength of the male Subconscious can become difficult to handle when the female Subconscious he joins has difficulty with his overwhelming strength.

Because of this, many times human beings continue to fight within themselves—with what and who they are, what they are doing, and why they are doing it—without recognizing that they are being carefully guided and directed. They are being fulfilled on all levels, especially those Subconscious Minds who are from outer space who find it difficult to understand that they are here to help, to teach, and to bring good and very wonderful understanding to the world—not just to their own particular human.

Because of this, sometimes actions that take place seem very wrong to the humans, until they recognize, for some reason or another, that these activities that have changed their lives or have made their lives different in many ways are rightful. At that point, because Karma/Dharma has been handled in many instances, it is very important for the human to recognize it as a new beginning—something else that is going to take place which sometimes requires changes of energy within the subconscious area.

Thus, humans must begin to allow things to happen, to work with the Karma/Dharma, not against it, to find that within every action there is a reaction *rightfully*, sometimes not always acceptable, but rightfully placed. Therefore, the results from these situations become a betterment for the life of the person and also for the Subconscious fulfillment of their Karma/Dharma, which they have brought forth.

Many humans cannot quite yet accept this kind of understanding—that their Subconscious is in charge, that they are working for it, like in a job, and they have to work towards fulfilling the job they have accepted when they came into life.

Within this, you begin to understand that your purpose has great beauty and fulfillment, not just for you, not even just for your Subconscious Awareness, but for the fulfillment of purpose that is far beyond that which is the single action of the time you live now. It is part of many past lives of different humans who have been instruments for the same subconscious area that brings you and others into life to do the work. Are you understanding this purpose?

**Comment:** *When we look at average human beings, their beliefs don't seem to be so much with regard to their Subconscious Minds but rather the authority of the outside world. That seems to be where they draw their strength from.*

**EC:** That is true. Because as time goes on, the child at first is not totally aware that it is acting out, like on a stage, in someone else's garment, and sometimes the child refuses to listen, becoming recalcitrant and doing many things that cause the situation to become overwhelming. But as the child matures, it begins to see that there is some kind of purpose in everything it does and this helps it to work for and with the Subconscious. That is the belief you have in what and who you are in these particular situations. It is always there—whether you know it or not.

At this point, it is imperative that each one recognizes that their Subconscious has chosen their parents for their strengths and weaknesses and their genes. Thus, each one comes in with some kind of weakness or strength that they have to totally and completely use to bring about balance and security in their lives, as well as the lives of those who are working with the Dharma and those who are part of a pattern in which Karma has become a fulfilling activity.

If you understand this, it helps you to move through situations that many times seem overwhelming or wrong to you, until you recognize, somehow or another as you move through it, that there is some purpose, a Sacred Purpose, that you have not yet learned, but must learn in order to fulfill that Sacred Purpose.

**Comment:** *I do understand this, and that these are the teachings coming from my Subconscious.*

**EC:** When you talk to your Subconscious Minds and communicate with them, many times that which seems wrong or not rightful becomes very clear and helpful because you have communicated with self— not with someone outside of you necessarily, but self, which is what Luke has said: "Physician, heal thyself"— though it is not physicians in this case, but human beings healing themselves from within, not from outside themselves.

Comment: *I know these teachings create a tremendous upheaval and a transition into something new that enables me to go on, even though my Consciousness does struggle against the Subconscious Minds in accepting "their will."*

EC: Working with and communicating with the Subconscious is a beautiful method to learn lessons and to become totally aware that you are doing a good job or sometimes failing to do a job. You do not understand that until you go within and learn from within yourself—not from someone outside who will help to guide but not give you the answers that your self does.

# Step 2

## Acceptance

- *It is necessary for you to accept that you are an instrument, expressing the wonderful, carefully planned work of your Subconscious Minds—your Basic Selves.*

- *In doing this work, you are not expressing what you usually regard as your own mind or your free will. Rather, you are expressing the plan of your Subconscious Minds and High Self.*

- *Accepting and expressing the action of this plan can bring you satisfaction and fulfillment.*

**Eternal Cosmos:** At this point, I enter in peace and love, blessing each one of you to be part of this very important knowledge and wisdom from higher realms and inner space, in the great beauty of the fulfillment of the Creator's Grace.

The factor that is most important at this point is *Acceptance*. Acceptance is very different from any other kind of creative essence that has been part of this work. It is most unique, in that it works with the past, the present, and the future, which involves humans becoming instruments through the beautiful and very wonderful work of their own inner minds, their inner selves—their Basic Selves.

It is necessary at this point that each one *accept* this as something that has been very carefully planned. However, many humans feel their own mind is in charge and therefore do not always accept that their Subconscious Minds are actually in charge.

The Subconscious Minds are that which give one the right to use the work that the Subconscious Minds have very carefully researched in the Akashic Records about their particular past memories of many different lifetimes—sometimes over many millions of years.

*The action then means acceptance that you are an instrument for the Subconscious Minds* to place you into a fulfillment of their particular purpose—to complete, with the High Self, what you have come in to work out in their memories, in the memory bank of past lives.

Sometimes it seems difficult for human beings to accept that they are motivated not by their own minds or their free will, but by a different kind of acceptance—the fact that each one comes in to be of use to humanity, collectively and individually.

Please know that your acceptance of this particular way of looking at and activating this plan becomes something which brings you satisfaction and fulfillment. And when you leave life and go into Spirit, you look back and know that you have definitely been of great use, not only to self, family, and friends, but to the very great beauty of the wisdom and knowledge of that which is within you.

Many of you at this point are beginning to accept, to totally and completely understand, this great beauty and the challenges. Parents are chosen rightfully by the human's Subconscious to teach; to bring about strength, not weakness; and to bring help in every way to fulfill the particular Karmic/Dharmic plan of the Subconscious.

Do understand that this is a step in the direction in which fulfillment becomes part of your own particular plan, through the Subconscious and human acceptance, to fulfill the past, the present, and to very definitely make way for a good future up ahead.

# Step 3

## Communication

- *Understanding the pattern of these teachings is very important. In order to acquire this understanding, communication with your Subconscious Minds is necessary.*

- *Strength and fulfillment will be one result of this communication—for you personally and also for people, places, and activities with which you are involved.*

- *This communication will also help you understand many other things, including why certain experiences—particularly those that are difficult—come into your life.*

**Eternal Cosmos:** The pattern of this particular schoolhouse is filled with unique areas of understanding. It is most important that each one who becomes aware of the teaching of the Fellowship learn how to understand the pattern of teaching.

Within the pattern, understanding becomes important, but not quite as important as *Communica-*

43

*tion, for you cannot understand until you communi-*
*cate with the very great and wonderful wisdoms of the*
*Subconscious Minds—the Male / Female Basic Selves.*

First of all, your Subconscious Minds have come
forward in many, many lifetimes hoping to fulfill the
plan given to them by the Creative Source. The Subconscious Minds have come to bring into the world of
reality that which could work for them and with
them to fulfill this plan—through their communication with you and your communication with them.

Many times people come into this work without
realizing they are instruments of their Subconscious
Minds. Therefore, it is difficult for them to finally
understand that this life is an important area of
finishing work of past subconscious memories, so the
present and the future can be fulfilled and fulfilling.

To determine what needs to be finished, the Subconscious Minds research the Akashic Records—not
of the person, for the person changes in each life, but
of that which is involved with their own particular
subconscious memory bank of what they have done or
not done—Karma and Dharma from their past lives.

Therefore, as each of you becomes involved with
your life situations, you must understand that you
become an important element in their fulfillment.
The Subconscious Minds do all they can to make this
fulfillment as easy as possible—though many times

not realizing either that the human does not understand why such things are happening, or the human
does not understand how to make them better.
Therefore, it is important that each of you communicate with your Inner Selves to gain this understanding.

Many children do this long before they grow into
adulthood and know very well that there were
those—their Subconscious Minds—who came into
their lives in the beginning talking to them, teaching
them, helping them many times to overcome areas in
their lives that did not seem to be working right—
areas involved with family, with schools, and with
friends or lack of friends.

All of these areas are involved with the Subconscious Awareness that the child seemed to have a
better opportunity to reach than the adult. Adults
often close down these doorways of true understanding and do not believe or do not accept that which is
part of the Three Selves teaching.

*Therefore, we ask you to communicate with your
Subconscious Awareness by simply listening and
going within.*

Also, remember that as you reach yourself, for
that is what it is, you are already involved with the
pattern of making your life better through accepting
the fact that you have come in to be of help to many—

not just to yourself, but to many you are with—and to become totally involved with the areas of the Subconscious Awareness.

Sometimes the humans become very irritated, angry that they are being used, or misused, not realizing they are being strengthened, they are being given help—not only from within, but from that which is teaching them.

Each area which seems to be overcoming them, to be overwhelming, is a schoolhouse, a teaching process, when it becomes fully understood. Then the situation either becomes finished, or many times the humans decide not to do it, not to complete it, and they quit.

Therefore, we ask you to know full well that all humans have come in with a purpose, not for themselves alone, but for the fulfillment of a vast number of many different memories, in which each past life has a purpose and each person has a reason for returning Karmically, or with the Dharma of helping others.

Do communicate with yourself—with your Subconscious! It will help you a great deal when you hear or sense the inner voice within your mind and especially in your dreams. You will find that much of what you learn strengthens and fulfills you.

*Communication* is the third step—communication with your Subconscious Minds. The fourth step, *Understanding*, becomes totally involved with what you *do* with your communication.

# Step 4

## Understanding

- *Understanding is necessary in order to learn what your purpose in this lifetime is.*

- *Dealing with life's troublesome issues is easier if you understand the reasons behind them—reasons that often originated in other lifetimes.*

- *You must understand that the Subconscious is teaching you, the human instrument, how to strengthen yourself and how to overcome the past.*

- *Through these teachings, you can understand the processes that continually move you closer to accomplishing your Sacred Purpose.*

---·∗·---

**Eternal Cosmos:** We will now give you the fourth step, which we hinted at in the last step: *Understanding.*

49

When you understand your purpose—your reason for being on the planet or in the life force—it becomes easier to handle the various actions that each one of you is going through at this time, whether patterns of health, jobs, personal involvement with family and mates, or any other actions.

Everything seems in some way to be heavily impacted at this point by something unknown that appears to be overwhelming many people, to the point that they are depressed and totally unaware they are working through Karma/Dharma. These actions are not for themselves alone, but also for their subconscious memory bank that—coming in from many, many different lifetimes, male and female—brings a whole new involvement and attitude and activity into the purpose for which the humans have been brought into this lifetime.

Because working through Karma/Dharma is oftentimes overwhelming to humans, they have the right to leave if they wish, and some do. When they stay and work it out and overcome that which seems to be overwhelming, they become aware of *understanding* why they have been brought into the life plan to help, not just themselves as humans, but to help a subconscious memory bank of many different lifetimes, so the good these humans do—their Dharma—becomes service to help others overcome their own Karma. But other actions of Karma become that which, in many ways, causes humans to be unable to totally accept that they, in their own way, have failed to correct past errors that caused them to be overwhelmed in this lifetime.

Overwhelming actions can be understood totally if one accepts the fact that humans are working out that which is a teaching, not just for themselves, but for others—learning to become part of many different kinds of understanding of that which has brought them into the plan through these various memories of other lives in which they, the humans, have not been present, but their Subconscious Minds have.

The teaching here begins to clarify each step, so the human beings can understand the reason, see the purpose, and continuously become involved with that which gives them a feeling of accomplishment, which is important in every lifetime—accomplishing that which is called their *Sacred Purpose*.

Each of you, and others like you, come into a schoolhouse such as this to learn a new method of overcoming the past so it becomes a better future— not just a better present, but a better future. Many human beings are learning through this method to understand that what they think is failure is not truly *their* failure, but the action of the subconscious plan they have come in to fulfill—to be of great good, not only to themselves and their human world, but to many people who are part of the Karma/Dharma they work with and for.

Each of you has, at this point, become increasingly aware that your actions become bettered, fulfilling, and fulfilled through various struggles that many find difficult to handle—learning that in struggling one becomes strengthened.

When the human being at birth is in the custody of parents, who are chosen by the Subconscious to work through these various methods and memories, it becomes something which strengthens the human. This enables the parents to teach their children and other children how to overcome the past, so the present and the future become bettered, not only for them but for everyone else they are involved with.

Each of you has this memory within you that is part of something which, by understanding it, helps you become better, more competent, and more accepting of the teaching and the subconscious plan.

Do understand that no one is trying to punish you—only trying to teach you how to strengthen yourself by overcoming the past to become totally aware that your Subconscious gains and becomes better, heightened, and more aware.

Thus you, too—within your mind, body, and Spirit—become bettered and increase your value to others around you, even to the people you sometimes find difficult to be involved with. But by learning how to work with your Subconscious, by understanding its purpose, you become fulfilled and fulfilling.

# Step 5

## Sensitivity

- *Your inborn sensitivity—your intuition—will bring you guidance and direction to overcome uncertainty, and it will answer your questions about your human purpose.*

- *You operate from your own subconscious memory patterns, which are accessible through your sensitivity.*

- *Sensitivity will show you that the Subconscious Minds, not your everyday Conscious self, are often directing your mind, thoughts, and actions.*

- *Sensitivity will equip you to teach others, so they too can understand and appreciate their true relationship to life and each other.*

**Eternal Cosmos:** This step will bring about a teaching and knowledge that is difficult for many of you to fully understand, which is this—*you are not always in charge of your own mind and your own actions, and you don't always have complete conscious*

*awareness that what you think, act, and do is exactly
what your Subconscious Minds believe is correct and
right.*

You are being led and directed. You are in a
schoolhouse in which your Subconscious Minds have
researched the Akashic Records for past-life involvements. This has brought each one of you in with a
Subconscious Awareness, using the strengths and
weaknesses of parents, to complete the action of
either service and Dharma to someone or of fulfilling
and completing a past action that is unfinished in the
subconscious areas—Karma.

Accepting this requires a certain amount of
understanding, and using your *Sensitivity* is the next
step—the sensitivity that each one of you, as a
human being, has brought with you through the
Subconscious Awareness.

Now is the time for each of you, through this
sensitivity, to recognize that you are part of a very
wonderful teaching in which you will learn that when
you work with your Subconscious Awareness, you
become fulfilled, in your own way, to fulfill the future
as well as the past and the present.

Each one of you has a great amount of knowledge
which has not yet been tapped. *By being sensitive to
your Subconscious Minds*—by reaching to them when
you have questions, when you find you do not know

whether you are in the right place or the right action or whether it is rightful for you to be involved as an instrument for someone else beside yourself—*you will receive your own answers.*

Your sensitivity, what you call your *intuition*, is definitely part of the plan that helps you to accept and understand that this is something you totally and completely accepted before birth, or you would not be in this human plan.

Those who are not willing to be involved with their Subconscious Minds' ideals, ideas, or activities can very quickly move away from them if they wish. But if they accept them, they then can find that within the work—within their particular plan—they are able to learn and heighten their Spiritual Awareness. Humans can become aware of their Subconscious Minds, which, in their own way, are teaching and giving them help to be someone in a different image, yet still retain their own image in the world of reality.

Each human can find this will be the best and very greatest way to learn how to work with self, to be able in many ways to heal and help self, and to fulfill self within the subconscious area.

Each of you have come in to do this, and whether you have accepted it or not is up to you. For in spite of everything, you will learn from this kind of work how to deal with everyone, including your own self, within a plan that gives you teaching, knowledge, and wisdom that is truly your own sensitivity—your own intuition—filled with great beauty of the past, the present, and the future.

Accepting and knowing that you are an instrument and within a plan, you can learn and teach this to others so they know—when they are helping or serving in Dharma or when they are completing the Karma—that it is part of something they have earned, not necessarily gained, but earned through the use of the Subconscious, since the human is the instrument the Subconscious uses.

Sometimes it is very heavy and overwhelming. But if you use your sensitivity—your intuitive power—to speak to your own self to find out exactly what the reason or purpose is, you will find that you begin to express in a way that is not going to make you different or unusual. Your Subconscious Minds can fulfill the plan, not only for themselves but for yourself as an instrument of great beauty and Light.

# Step 6

## Service

- *You are here to be of service to your Subconscious Minds—through aligning yourself with them, your High Self, your Teachers and Guides, and your Super-Consciousness.\**

- *Your service, performed with strength, courage, determination, and a willingness to learn, will bring you knowledge and wisdom you would not gain in any other way.*

- *The service for which you have been chosen will bring great good to others as well as to yourself. Knowing this can make the lessons in your life more acceptable.*

**Eternal Cosmos:** The pattern of this particular work becomes more and more involved with your Subconscious Awareness, which is causing what is happening to you as part of a plan.

\* *See the Field of Consciousness chart opposite page 1.*

*Service is what the Subconscious Minds expect of you,* and they ask you to communicate with them—as we have said in the previous steps—because it is imperative, at this point in the world you live in, that everyone realize that service is the area you have come in to work with—service for the Higher Mind, for the greater beingness of the Super-Consciousness, your High Self, your Subconscious Minds, and your Teachers and Guides.

The service they have brought you in to work with, as their instrument, is that which they have failed to fulfill in past lives on the subconscious level. It is a beautiful, wonderful service that gives each one the right to take a particular plan and work with it for the good of humanity.

You have found yourself many times wondering why you are here, why you are doing things—because you have not been told, unless it was through a teaching of this kind, why you have become involved with many different kinds of problems, many different kinds of activities, which don't seem to make sense. If you have the courage, determination, and willingness to learn from it all, it becomes a schoolhouse of great beauty, in which you become bettered, fulfilled, and definitely gain a pattern of knowledge and wisdom that would not be gained in any other way except through service.

Only through courage and determination can you become of service—not only to those in your life now, but to those who come in the future. Your Subconscious Minds bring them all forward, for you and them to become part of this particular unusual, unique way of fulfilling a plan.

Each one is learning from this school of thought that—first as you live it and then as you teach it— you, as an instrument, become more and more aware of the beauty and fulfillment of this service to complete Karma/Dharma.

If, within this service, you choose to leave, feeling you cannot handle the situation, not understanding it, not in any way knowing you are doing something good, it becomes rightful for you to leave. But remember that the Subconscious returns in another lifetime with another human instrument to fulfill the plan.

Acceptance is a very important area, but it is important also to understand that your service is of great good, not only to others but to yourself. Your understanding makes it much more manageable for you to learn the lessons you are being taught through this schoolhouse—very definitely a work of great beauty and fulfillment. You will find that as you become Love and Light, as you become understanding and compassionate about that which is happening to you in many different forms of activity—sometimes not good, sometimes that which you cannot handle—your Subconscious helps you, with the loving and caring of the female and the beautiful wisdom and knowledge of the male.

Do accept that you have been chosen! Accept it. If you do that, already it is half the battle. You will find this to be true.

# Step 7

## Fulfillment of Purpose

- *Among the ten steps, Fulfillment of Purpose is the most important, because the human instrument has been chosen to fulfill the purpose of the Subconscious Minds.*

- *As you work to fulfill your purpose, you are like a performer on stage who puts on a costume and plays a certain role.*

- *The role you play may seem strange, overwhelming, or in error, yet you will make it your own when you realize you are here to serve, to fulfill the purpose of the Subconscious Awareness.*

**Eternal Cosmos:** The past lives of the Subconscious Awareness are taken from the Akashic Records and brought forward to fulfill both Karma and Dharma.

Humans come in believing they are in charge, but know before the end of their lifetime that many times they are motivated and activated in *Fulfillment of*

*Purpose* in ways which do not always seem to fit into what humans believe is their plan.

Sometimes it becomes very difficult to accept that in these ten steps—and *all* the steps are necessary to fulfill this work—*the action of fulfillment of purpose is the most important.*

Many times we, the Teachers, work with people to make it evident that each one of them is in a kind of drama or comedy, in which they put on someone else's clothes to act out a role in certain activities. This is very much what is present here in fulfillment of purpose, for you are, each one, an actor or actress on the stage and you are working for the purpose, the action, which is fulfillment of purpose from your subconscious memory bank.

Humans come in totally and very much involved with doing these actions, because they already accepted, before entering life, that they were part of a particular plan. Because they all have come in totally and completely to do this, many times it is difficult for the mind of humans—not the Subconscious Minds, but the Conscious mind of humans—to accept that they are working for someone else, not themselves. But as time goes on, many of these activities become very much involved with fruition, fulfillment, and plans that bring each one into balance and security.

It is very important that each one flow with this chosen life plan, knowing that within the pattern—no matter how strange or overwhelming it often is for humans to have to accept something that does not seem to be their plan—it *becomes* their plan when they realize they are here for service and fulfillment of purpose in every sense of the word.

Do know that you are doing great good when you help your Subconscious Minds, because you are helping *yourself* to accept and understand that you have come in willingly to accept a particular fulfillment of purpose.

# Step 8

## Faith

- *Faith in your Subconscious Minds will help you overcome the challenges of this lifetime.*

- *To have faith simply means to have trust—in your <u>Selves</u>, which include your Subconscious Minds, your Conscious Awareness and High-Self Awareness, and your Teachers and Guides.*

———••❖••———

**Eternal Cosmos:** Each one needs to understand that this work has been on the planet for many eons of time. But it always gets pushed back into the past rather than brought forward into the future, because many people cannot accept this unique approach to the self—that the mind you come in with as a human being is not what, on the conscious level, you learn it is. It is also your subconscious male and female— your Inner Selves—working with your High-Self Awareness and your Teachers and Guides to bring actions into being, and you help them do this to fulfill the past, the present, and the future.

The eighth step is *Faith*—trust in your Inner Selves that they will help you overcome the challenges they have brought forward for you to bring into balance . . . that which, within your human self, becomes your work with them, and their work not only with you but with the world, and all of that which is involved with wisdom, knowledge, and fulfillment.

Therefore, faith in yourself and your Subconscious Minds must be understood as the only way the challenge of this particular work can be fulfilled, that it can be handled in a way that makes each of you aware that you have much more *within you* than you totally comprehend.

Know that this is the time and place to bring forth this work—from the past and the present into the future. Each of you will become aware then that you are part of the changes in this New Age that will bring forth a different understanding of self and of the challenges that are given to you that are not yours totally, but belong to the Inner Selves who work with you to bring about balance, security, and fulfillment.

# Step 9

## Strength, Courage, and Determination

- *Personal strength, courage, and determination are required as you move toward the accomplishment of your Sacred Purpose.*

- *These virtues are essential for you to work successfully with the Subconscious Minds in achieving fulfillment—fulfillment for the Subconscious Minds themselves, for yourself, and for others.*

——————•••᠅•••——————

**Eternal Cosmos:** What is important to understand is that every step has a certain amount of knowledge for each person. As you believe and accept the steps that are placed before you in this unique approach to your past lives, you understand how your subconscious area, your present, and your future are all part of your particular plan.

*Strength, Courage, and Determination*, together, are the ninth step—a trinity of purpose in which you must know you are working not just for yourself in your own human areas and understanding, but for your subconscious pattern that is bringing forth these great and wonderful steps. *Each step will bring you into a fulfillment of your own Sacred Purpose and that of the Subconscious Minds.* All of these steps require strength, courage, and determination to fulfill your Sacred Purpose.

Each one of you must understand that you have come in completely accepting the fact that you are part of a very important step-by-step plan in which— through strength, courage, and determination—you fulfill yourself as a human and also fulfill the subconscious memory, in which Karma and Dharma bring forth these wonderful areas of helping and healing—not only of yourself in this activity but of everyone you come in contact with.

That is not just part of this lifetime but of many other memories, whether the human remembers them or not. They are all parts of a particular plan that brings each one into each lifetime in a different human body to fulfill their Body, Mind, and Spirit. The purpose is to fulfill and bring into balance and security the Subconscious Awareness that they— totally and completely guided by the High Self and the blessed Creator—have come in to fulfill, in areas of the past, present, and future.

Each step then becomes a very great and wonderful manifestation of that which is strength in your own mind as well as in the minds of the Subconscious. Each step is also involved with a very beautiful acceptance that humans have come in to be instruments for a great and wonderful plan to help the planet, individually and collectively, through strength, courage, and determination.

Do know that each one has come in with the great knowledge that they have been, not themselves as a human but as an instrument, always working in coordination and cooperation with the subconscious memory bank and the Akashic Records of the past. That which is in each of your lifetimes—in re-embodiment in a new body, a new activity, a new situation—brings this forth into fulfillment.

Know that you are accomplishing everything through your own personal understanding of strength, courage, and determination to do so.

# Step 10

## Fulfillment of Karma and Dharma

- *Your fundamental purpose in this lifetime is to work with the Subconscious Minds to fulfill your Karma (by overcoming your past failures) and your Dharma (by helping others through service to fulfill their Karma).*

- *Working with your purpose is easier when you recognize that you are helping to bring your life and the lives of others to completion and fulfillment.*

- *Accepting your purpose accomplishes great good, individually and collectively.*

------••❖••------

**Eternal Cosmos:** These steps we are presenting are part of that which each human moves through when going into the world of the future, finding them more helpful when they are fully explained and understood.

This tenth step is acceptance of involvement with *Fulfillment of Karma and Dharma*—for others as well as self—to help the Subconscious Minds fulfill their Life Plan in this particular lifetime.

Those humans who have already accepted and understood this work and knowledge will find that their acceptance and understanding allows them to move more easily through the areas of Karma and Dharma. Those humans are helping to fulfill their plan as instruments for the Subconscious Minds and to assist the Subconscious Minds to correct Karmic errors of the past. Dharma is service on the part of the human to the Subconscious Minds to fulfill and complete what the Subconscious Minds failed to complete for others in the past.

This is helping the Subconscious Minds, through their Karma/Dharma, to learn, to understand, to know, and to really believe that each human is useful to accomplish a purpose of great beauty, to fulfill a plan in every way.

Many humans at first, not knowing they are being used as instruments of the Subconscious Minds, become threatened that their own mind, their own actions, their own will is not always useful, and either accept, resist, or retreat. Therefore, humans will accept only what they wish to accept and become more aware that—within the act of helping the Subconscious Awareness of the past with Karma, which is to overcome past failures, and with Dharma, or service, which is to help others do so—they each have become very great instruments, not only for themselves but for the Creative Source that has helped humans become aware of their useful purpose to assist the Subconscious Minds.

*Please accept that all humans are doing something of great good,* not only for those who are part of this particular plan but those who will be of use to a future plan—since, when the subconscious actions are finished and completed in this lifetime, new ideals and ideas become part of the Subconscious Minds.

Many are not aware of how much good is done in a lifetime—including to those in their family and environment—by the human's cooperation with the Subconscious Minds to bring situations to a head, to finish and conclude patterns that are rightful and have become fulfilled—similar to a play, in which the actor or actress moves through these "comedies and dramas" to bring about balance, security, and hope for a completion of the Karmic Patterns—and also earns Dharma by helping others complete their Karma.

Every human, at any given moment, has many patterns of subconscious Karma/Dharma needing attention and action. These patterns may occur one after the other or they may overlap. Some are just beginning, some are ongoing, some are ending. They may require long or short periods of time to work through. They may be easy or difficult. But patterns of one kind of another are always in progress.

So here, in the tenth step, you have that which is the conclusion of a pattern of the past to fulfill Karma and Dharma. The tenth step is to recognize that by doing so, you are fulfilling the Sacred Purpose, not only of the Subconscious Minds but of that which is the fulfillment of all that no longer has any reason to be brought forward again. Once Karma and Dharma are accepted and fulfilled, the pattern of the past is concluded.

# Applying the Three Selves Concepts

# 4

## The Importance of Discipline

**Eternal Cosmos:** A most important area that human beings, as instruments, need to recognize within their Karmic and Dharmic plan—which has been placed into the Subconscious Awareness—is *Discipline*, in word and deed.

Many human beings are not capable of understanding that the disciplines of various Eastern concepts—of those who live within areas of disciplined involvement with prayer, Light, and fulfillment—are part of the way they fulfill their plan, and that they often find answers simply by quietly disciplining themselves to listen.

But you do not quite yet understand why certain very unusual situations become part of your life, your plan, your healing, and your lack of healing. You do not see it as a fulfillment of the plan when disciplines are forced upon you if there is an error in your mind, body, or spirit.

Each of you has come in totally aware that this is
the job you asked for, whether you remember it or
not. The Subconscious Minds, then, process whatever
you have to do through disciplining each of you in
simple actions that sometimes are uncomfortable,
unhappy, and many times seem not to end. The
Subconscious Minds may even increase that involvement with the human being to a point where the
human no longer wishes to stay or to be part of the
plan.

Discipline, however, is part of that which each of
you must recognize helps you. Through these various
forms of "attack" on the body, mind, and spirit, the
disciplines you learn—either in your religion, school,
home, or from your parents—give you a disciplinary
pattern which makes you understand that through
that particular plan, situations are completed and
fulfilled.

Each of you becomes strengthened, knowing that
with the disciplining of your own mind and body,
actions which many times seem hopeless become
hopeful because of what you have learned through
whoever teaches you—parents, teachers in school, or
those in different kinds of religious backgrounds in
which the disciplines of prayer and Light become
evident and fulfilling.

We ask you to recognize that discipline is an
important action. Each of you has come in to fully

accept that what you are doing is not totally your own plan, but the plan your Subconscious has carefully analyzed before you entered, giving you parents with needed strengths and weaknesses, and giving you the ability to know and understand that you are being disciplined in a way that gives you the right to fulfill the plan of the Subconscious, whether it seems rightful to you as a human or not.

Please understand that discipline is not always that which overwhelms. Sometimes it gives a perfect example to humans, so within their careful analysis and understanding that they are part of a plan, even though it seems unreal and overwhelming, many times the end result *is* something very great within the plan—through religion, through stress within families, through areas in which many of the experiences in childhood and maturity become the fulfillment and completion of Karma and Dharma within the plan of the Subconscious Minds.

**Question:** *One of the steps of working with the Three Selves is "Fulfillment of Purpose." Another is "Fulfillment of Karma and Dharma." Can you elaborate on the difference between them?*

EC: Fulfillment of purpose is not exactly your own particular fulfillment. It is your fulfillment of purpose of that which has brought you in to be the instrument for the Subconscious Minds. Many people do not know what that purpose is until they live through it. Sometimes it becomes very difficult to live through it, and many quit and run away rather than to complete the action.

Fulfillment of Karma and Dharma is fulfillment of purpose in a different sense, because within the disciplines we have talked about, human beings find they are completing activities, fulfilling Karma and Dharma, without even knowing it is being done.

Sometimes humans question: "Why? Why? Why?" And yet, when the final result becomes evident, Karma and Dharma are the result of that which *is* fulfillment of purpose, becoming totally involved with that particular activity. Remember that you have come in fully accepting on the subconscious level, whether you know it or not, whatever is happening to you—sometimes accepting it on the conscious level and sometimes not, sometimes being overwhelmed, sometimes not—and if you run away from it, it becomes again the same Karma you have not released and not completed in other lifetimes.

Each time you come in as a different human being with the same particular activity to fulfill, the same Karma or Dharma, you become stronger, more able to handle it. And each time, it becomes the beauty of fulfillment of purpose.

Q: *With regard to discipline, what about daily rituals as part of spiritual practice?*

EC: Spiritual practice is a discipline that many of the Eastern religions, not really becoming involved with what you call Karma and Dharma, take as their particular approach, knowing that within their Subconscious Awareness, the only way to fulfill their plan is to have discipline and ritual. Ritual then becomes their way of life, which is rightful for them because they come in with a different understanding of what Karma and Dharma are. Therefore, it becomes a disciplining of their body, mind, and spirit in order to fulfill what the Subconscious has brought them in for—to provide them with these areas that make them totally aware they must assist within their life plans through the discipline of ritual.

Our work is not like anyone else's concepts, such as other religious teachings. Notice that many religions become rigid in disciplining their members, to the point that the members many times lose the opportunity to understand why they are present, simply knowing they have been placed into an action which is considered discipline—rather than religion or that which is the useful purpose of love and fulfillment of purpose.

Q: *Then are we in the Western world working through Karma and Dharma through action, rather than through spiritual discipline and ritual?*

EC: This is part of the very definite memory of "tribal disciplines" of the past, in which the tribe was able to make laws that disciplined the human beings into activities they did not like or want. This was because the tribe made the laws, just like your government makes laws. Sometimes your governmental activities become rigidly involved with what the government wants, not what your Subconscious wants. But you still have to comply with the disciplining of the government, so you have to look at it as part of the same kind of fulfillment of purpose.

# 5

## How to Work with Yourself

**Eternal Cosmos:** I enter in peace and bless you, each one. We are here simply to give you a short lesson on speaking to your Teachers, because it is important that you begin to know how to work with yourself.

We suggest, as one method, using *hypnotherapy,* because that gives you answers from your inner minds—your Subconscious Minds. We want you to realize that whenever you feel depressed, anxious, angry, or misused, and your Karma is not what you want, or you are not in any way willing or anxious to be involved with what is happening to you, you need to realize that you took on a task when you entered this lifetime. That task gives you the right to have help from those who, whether you like it or not, are in charge of your life—your Subconscious Minds—*if you communicate with them*! If you confer with them. If you listen to what they can tell you about the Karma, the Dharma, the actions that are happening.

So instead of looking outside of yourself at someone you think is harming you, instead of looking to
see what is invading or in some way destroying you,
please look within yourself. Talk to yourself as if you
were talking to a very fine Teacher and Guide. In so
doing, you will find that your Subconscious Minds
and your High Self will begin to give you the lessons
you have come in to learn and fulfill. You have simply
come in as an instrument for that which is the great
and beautiful work of the past, the present, and the
future.

Please remember that you are here, not for
yourself alone, but for every collective and individual
action of the past—not of yourself, not of you as a
person, but as that which you have been within the
image of the Subconscious Awareness. Learn to speak
to your Subconscious Minds. Learn to communicate
with them, as they are your primary Teachers and
Guides.

You will find you can get many answers from
yourself that you cannot get from other people. The
Subconscious Minds want *you*—for you are their
instrument—to talk to them. They will not always
give other people the answer for you, or they may
give other people a Karmic answer, or an answer you
cannot understand.

**Question:** *If I understand correctly, you are
saying that if any of us go through a traumatic*

*experience, our job is to ask the Basic Selves—
the Subconscious Minds—what that experience
represents and what we need to realize and
understand more than anything else. Is that
what you mean by a lesson?*

EC: Correct! The point is that it is not *your* lesson.
You are simply acting out the pattern for the Subconscious Minds that brought you in to work for them, to
act for them, to bring them into balance and fulfillment.

Some people become very concerned that nothing
is happening totally correctly within what they
believe should happen. Many times the humans, past
and present, find it very difficult to feel they are
being handled correctly or helped. Yet they are not
aware that everything given to them from their
Subconscious Awareness is from a broad scope of
memories in which each awareness of that memory
brings them into a fulfillment, a knowledge, and
help—not for self alone but for the tribal memory of
many that have been part of the past. Please accept
that each person has come in for a task that is not
always pleasant, is not always happy, and does not
always cause one to feel that something is being
accomplished through what is being done.

Remember that even if you become aware of the
importance of the communication with your Subconscious Minds and ask them questions, you can still go

to a psychic, a sensitive, a medium, but you will find
that they repeat and give you the same answer that,
whether you know it or not, you would get from
yourself. This means that your Teachers and Guides
are always there to help you. *Please realize this is a
lesson to teach and to learn from.*

**Q:** *Does this mean if I am aware that what I am
going through is not really for me personally but
for the Basic Selves—the Subconscious Minds—
to work out their Karma/Dharma, it will help
me to detach from a traumatic experience?*

**EC:** Yes, that is why you should not be depressed or
anxious, why you should *have faith not fear*, because
your High Self will always reassure you and the
Creative Source will always give you an answer so
you will be able to understand what is happening.
Indeed, those who cannot do it for themselves should
seek help from hypnotherapy, which is an ancient
way of speaking to yourself with the assistance of
another person. Anyone who has had this experience
knows it is unique and very, very beautiful.

**Q:** *Does self-hypnosis work in this kind of situation?*

**EC:** Self-hypnosis does not always work, because self-
hypnosis takes you *out* of the body and not within.
You go outside hunting for answers someplace else.
You travel out of the body instead of going within.

Sometimes when meditation becomes self-hypnosis, you go outside of the body and you leave the psychic doors—the Chakras—open for invasion of entities that are not always positive.

**Comment:** *I have been told when I am doing inner work that information coming from either the High Self or the Subconscious can be altered—completely reversed even—by our emotional and mental filters, which can mistranslate the information. I am referring to accuracy in the interpretation of these communications.*

**EC:** They can be altered by your own mind through mistranslation. Sometimes an inaccuracy is a challenge to you, and is very definitely useful to make you understand the difference between right and wrong.

**Comment:** *There is also entity interference.*

**EC:** There are walk-ins that occur when you go into meditation and leave your psychic doors—your Chakras—open, or when your Spirit leaves to travel, to go to the High Self, or to go into another dimension. *You must always ask for protection and close the psychic doors before and after meditation!*

If you left your house to go on a trip, would you not lock your doors? You should think of it in that way. When you pray, talk to your Subconscious and say, *"If you are going to take me on a trip to get awareness, when I leave my home—my body—will you please close the psychic doors so nothing can get in until we get back?"* Talk to your Subconscious Minds and they will help you.

**Q:** *Are you saying that before we go within to listen, we should use the Fellowship's "Mantra Prayer of Protection"?\**

**EC:** Absolutely. Make sure you are totally aware that you are not going to leave any doors open for anything to enter.

**Comment:** *I have received accurate answers and inaccurate answers. If I was getting inaccurate answers, maybe it was because I was leaving my psychic doors open.*

**EC:** Not only that, but *because you <u>wanted</u> the answer you got, you accepted an answer that was inaccurate* rather than the accurate one.

Sometimes people do not believe what they hear, therefore they go outside, sometimes to another person—a psychic, a fortune teller, a sensitive, or someone who gives them an answer that pleases them more than the answer from within. That is part of what you must learn: to *discriminate* between the good and the bad, the accurate and the inaccurate. You, as the human being, must look at the whole

* *See page 141.*

situation from all angles to see how it could help or harm you.

Sometimes things happen to persons because they have to learn from them, and then learn to discriminate how to change them from wrong actions to right actions.

Many people become depressed and suicidal because they feel they are being harmed, that the world has treated them badly. But they do not realize they are working on a task that has everything they need in order to continue and to pattern themselves into that which *releases the past* and makes their present and future life better.

If they talk to their Subconscious—and also their High Self through their Subconscious—they will find they are being helped, healed, and supported. They will find that they have friends *within* rather than just friends on the outer. Many times people go within and know the answers are correct.

You must be able to analyze, to understand what the purpose is of the Subconscious Minds using you—though sometimes in your mind you think they are *misusing* you—until you have learned how to handle the situation for them, not just for self. This is a unique approach, very different, and will be very useful in the future to many.

**Q:** *How do I deal with an inaccurate communication?*

**EC:** If you mean a communication from the inside and you are not getting accurate answers, it means you are getting what you *want* to hear. For that reason, it is inaccurate to you. You have to learn to translate correctly. *You have to take an answer from within, look at it very carefully, then ask your Subconscious, "What's the purpose? What does that mean? Does that mean it is right or wrong? Help me to see the truth."* And, if necessary, go to someone like a hypnotherapist to find the part of yourself within that talks to you and who you can talk to. It is a very definite New Age pattern that many people have not yet used.

**Q:** *How can I tell if communication is accurate or not accurate? Can't I just ask my Subconscious, "If it's not accurate, even if I want to hear it, don't tell me"?*

**EC:** You can, but you must be discriminating and translate correctly, as we have recently explained. You have to learn to accept the challenge and work with it for its betterment—not for that which would harm you but for that which will help and teach you. It is a teaching.

Everything that happens to everyone on the planet Earth is a teaching. But if the Teachers are not good, then the answers are not good. So even if you have Teachers you trust, if they give you answers because you want to hear them, you have to challenge those answers to make sure you are getting correct answers for you—from your Subconscious as well as your outer self. It is very complicated, but you will also find it interesting and intriguing.

**Comment:** *This past year, I have found that if I am not satisfied or don't understand an answer, I can go to my High Self.*

**EC:** But you have to go *with* your Subconscious! Your High Self is there to help you, but the High Self does not usually in any way discard what the Subconscious has come to teach. They must cooperate with each other.

The High Self has brought the Subconscious in to choose you and your parents for their strengths and weaknesses, to help you—the human Consciousness—help them—the Subconscious. Therefore, many times there are patterns in which the Subconscious wants to rush things, wants to push things, and moves in directions that could be misunderstood, so the High Self then becomes very active in trying to make the Subconscious Minds realize they are pushing or jamming, and that is not rightful.

**Q:** *So are you saying that the High Self will generally be correct?*

**EC:** The High Self is *most* of the time—I said *most* of the time—correct. But many times the action is a "repeat" on the Subconscious level, which has caused the pattern to become part of the plan in order to be corrected. This means the Subconscious Minds are repeating something that must be changed and transmuted into something different. The High Self then has to help them fulfill that pattern.

**Comment:** *I understand that, at times, there are also disagreements between the High Self, the Master Teacher and Doctor Teacher, and the other Teachers.\**

**EC:** Yes, at times. The High Self simply sits there and watches and observes. If a disagreement arises, the High Self becomes a mediator to balance the situation, making sure that those who are condemning or condoning are able to accept and understand that which is being condemned or condoned. *That is the major area you must learn.* You must learn that within yourself is sometimes the repeat of a past mistake and therefore the High Self makes sure the Subconscious knows to learn from it.

**Q:** *So would the High Self discourage the Subconscious from making or repeating errors?*

* *See the Field of Consciousness chart opposite page 1.*

EC: The High Self would simply want the Subconscious Minds to know they have come to transmute something, not to continue it or to repeat it. Everyone has a wonderful High Self that will do anything to help the Subconscious Minds and their human instrument to overcome past errors and become fulfilled and complete the Karma/Dharma.

# 6

## Service to the Subconscious Awareness

**Eternal Cosmos:** Several interesting situations are becoming more prevalent within the pattern which is attempting to stop the Higher Realm from becoming part of what each of you has come to demonstrate: the plan to bring good, hope, help, and any other kind of gratitude.

We wish to point out that the Subconscious Minds have come in over and over again to bring humans into a plan that helps the humans learn, helps them succeed, helps them be fulfilled fully and completely within that which is the role of service—service to the Subconscious Awareness. That service makes it possible for each of you to become a healer, a helper, a pattern of good for all that is to come.

At this point, your planet is in deep trouble with that which is on the outside, attempting in some way to destroy the beauty of the heightened awareness in each of you. However, you become more and more aware that your Subconscious is not trying to destroy, but is trying in every way to bring about betterment for each one of you in your life plan.

It is important for each one of you to recognize that your life is increasing in value within the pattern of the Subconscious Awareness. Each of you has not known this to begin with and has just begun to learn this particular plan, so it is very difficult at times for the human mind to accept that it is not in full charge of making decisions, of doing all the things you are doing, and this sometimes does not seem to make sense.

When you are told by your Teachers and Guides that you are involved as an instrument, many of you cannot see it as a job well done. You have come to learn to live with it, to learn to work with it, to learn to accept it as part of the job you came to demonstrate, through and from the Subconscious Awareness.

Because each one of you, at this point, has different questions about this, it is imperative that you recognize that some of these situations are becoming more and more overwhelming to those who are not quite able to understand this purpose. Because each person has a different role to play, a different act to be involved with in their play, in their drama or their comedy, *it is _rightful_ that each of you question why these activities have come to you.*

Sometimes this knowledge comes not in your youth, when you could not understand it, but in your maturity. At that time, it becomes more and more a pattern that you understand is teaching you how to work with others as you are helped through being involved with your Subconscious Awareness in its "job well done." If you learn to work with your Subconscious Awareness, you will find that many of the things you look for in your life become evident when the Karma is completed and whole new areas of Life and Light become part of your activities and actions.

None of you are quite aware of how much you have already accomplished. You will find as time goes on that there are going to be many changes in the world you live in. And you will be able to handle them because you are being trained by an "inner voice," an inner area in which, when you ask questions of yourself, the answer comes clearly to help you promote the act of fulfillment of your very great purpose and that which is now part of the plan.

*We are asking you to recognize that your Subconscious Awareness works with you always.* But if you back off from the Karma/Dharma you came in to handle, feeling you do not want to be part of it, that is not wrong. It simply slows down the purpose, the reason for your being on the planet. And with that, your pattern more and more becomes one in which you quit before your time, or leave it before it is ready for you to leave. Or you do something that is not rightful for the fulfillment, not only of yourself but of the Karma and Dharma of the Subconscious. Remember that your Subconscious Minds have come in purposely to help you understand what you are doing for them and for yourself.

We ask you to remember this because many of you are going through stressful periods. Know this is true of everyone on the planet, not just you individually. Everyone is part of a tribal memory. Therefore, the tribe becomes part of those many areas in which your Subconscious needs you to fulfill the Karmic Plan— from the tribal memory as well as from individual memories.

You will find within the coming years that you learn much on your own within the plan that teaches you from this point of view. This is only the school-house. When you graduate with this particular knowledge or schoolhouse plan, you will find you are able to teach through your understanding of who you are, what you are here for, and whether or not you have accepted certain situations within the Subconscious Awareness.

**Comment:** *EC, it seems to me that one of the problems of the human condition is that we go through certain experiences and we have great difficulty interpreting those experiences.*

**EC:** *Interpretation* is something which, we have said over and over again, *requires your listening to your inner voice.*

You must understand that the Subconscious Minds cannot always tell you why or give you answers about why you are handling or mishandling situations, because within their own particular past memories, the same thing has occurred. Over and over again they come in trying to make up for that which has been a failure, or that which has in some other way become part of your plan with them to fulfill your Sacred Purpose.

Many people have already been given answers they could not quite believe—but their Subconscious had, in fact, answered their questions. Not with that which is words, or a voice, but that which promoted situations that brought balance and security to something which seemed impossible.

Many of you are already experiencing this, because you have accepted that this is a teaching process, and that when you have learned these lessons from your Subconscious Awareness, you will be able to help others. You will become the teacher through your Subconscious Awareness, so many others can begin to learn and fulfill the plan. *That is the purpose of this schoolhouse.*

Q: *This is an overall question. Why is the veil so thick, and we all want to get through it, and we all want to know the answers—but find it so difficult?*

EC: The pattern of the human world is that which is being taught by outer space. Many of you are not totally aware that you are not just human, but that you are part of another dimension, which has a different approach to situations. So the Subconscious must work with both your human self and that which is the outer-spacial self.

The outer-spacial selves come in with many different answers from past-life memory as well, but in their own way. It takes a longer time for the outer spacial beings to accept that they are part of the human world. They want everything to be like it was in another dimension, and that is not possible when you become the human being, to work out a plan.

The idea is to have patience and understanding with that which they are attempting to teach. When you go to school, at first you are not always able to understand. As time goes on, the teacher, in many different ways, gives you all the answers, but you must begin in your own particular mind and self to accept that these answers have value for you. That is the problem. Because the human being and the outer-spacial being do not always believe the Subconscious has the answers, they wait for certain other human beings, like psychics and fortune tellers, to give them answers. When they receive an answer that does not please them, they are lost. They do not know what to do.

So you must take everything you learn, every lesson, and place it into the understanding that will give you the best answer *from within*—so it will be accepted within yourself, from your Subconscious, which knows the right answer and will help you learn it eventually, if you have *patience and understanding*.

Comment: *EC, you have answered my question in a sense. But your answer is difficult to interpret because we have the human self pulling on us, we have the outer-spacial beings pulling on us, and we have all the other conflicts within Karma/Dharma that pull on us, and everything becomes confusing at times.*

EC: Not only that, but too many people are what you would call "psychic seekers." They go from one person to another to another, getting all kinds of answers that do not begin to make a balance, but only bring confusion. That is why, if you are feeling such confusion, we recommend that you sit quietly in a quiet place, have music if you wish in a quiet background— not anything that is rock-and-roll, but quiet music that balances you—and you will find that as you talk to yourself, the answers will come and you will begin to be part of the balancing-out of everything that is part of the plan.

It is your self that brings in these actions, but your self is definitely your Subconscious Self as well as your Conscious Self.

**Q:** *EC, is that part of psychic development?*

**EC:** Psychic development is good for some people. But some people, when they develop their psychic awareness, become more confused because they are getting answers from different areas—not only their own, but others—instead of listening carefully to what is within them in the intuitive quality of the Subconscious.

Teaching is very important—as long as you use it without controlling or without being controlled. When you learn certain lessons and they are controlling you to be only what *they* teach—and not what somebody else teaches, including your Self—it becomes very difficult for you to understand how to balance out the various confusions that follow.

**Q:** *Do the Subconscious Minds have an understanding of a person's mission? Or does the person have to teach the Subconscious that mission?*

**EC:** The mission is always present with the Subconscious, who cannot always make the human understand the mission but tries in many different ways to do so—sometimes making the human very confused as to what is missing or what is not missing, because humans have a different understanding than what the Subconscious is trying to teach them.

The point is to sit quietly and wait and listen to all the voices, so you can take the ones that suit and please you the most. For that is definitely your Subconscious Awareness helping you bring balance to your own particular plan. *Your Subconscious never pushes, never forces. It simply works with you to help you understand the Sacred Purpose that has brought you into a lifetime, and then it causes you to re-embody until that Sacred Purpose is completed.*

**Q:** *The Conscious Mind, then, is the one that sorts out all the information that comes through the Subconscious Minds?*

**EC:** The Subconscious has more understanding and knowledge than you can possibly know. But human beings are always so impatient to get through with the situation that they only listen to the part they wish to hear, and then sometimes it becomes less than reliable because it is not all of the answer, only part of it. That is the area of impatience about which, over and over again, the teachers tell you *patience, patience.* Be patient and you will find that if you have patience, your answers will come and the fulfillment of the Karma and Dharma will be completed, so you can finish the situation in this lifetime to go on to new ideals for the next generation.

**Q:** *With regard to what you just said, EC, what if we have different answers from different members of our teaching band, our Subconscious Minds, and we listen to all of them? You said to take the ones that suit and please us the most. What did you mean by that?*

**EC:** Choose the answer that deeply feels true and good and right to you. The point is that many people who are psychic seekers don't trust their own intuition or their own understanding of an answer, so they go to anyone who they think can tune in to what is happening. So they have about ten answers instead of one. They must choose which one pleases them.

Human beings must choose, then, and that's where this particular work is involved. Humans must choose what they feel will help them.

If they do not, then they must go back to their Subconscious to find out why, or what the reason is that the situation has not come to a conclusion. The Subconscious knows, but cannot force anything on anyone. When the time is right, the humans will accept that they are part of this difficult understanding of self. *Self is within you. Self is the answer within you.* If you ask others on the outside who do not truly know this and they give you answers that are rightful, but rightful in *their* own way, *those are their answers, not yours.* Then it becomes confusion.

**Comment:** *So EC, one of the Ten Steps that is involved with our teaching—having to do with the frame of reference—is "Acceptance." Acceptance means that if we truly acknowledge our Subconscious Minds, we stop being "psychic seekers" and really rely on ourselves as authorities to get our own answers.*

EC: Right! And you know that if you look back in your particular lifetime, each of you, no matter what you were taught, when you reached the point at which you wanted to "do it yourself"—the point at which you had to accept that you had the answer—many of you moved away from those of your family and your friends who told you differently, and you did so because you had heard the right answer from self.

# PSYCHIC CENTERS CHART (Chakras)

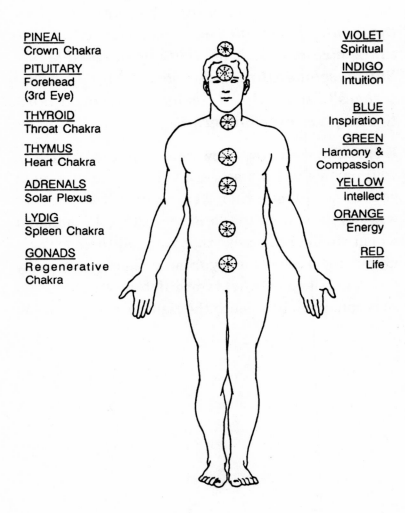

PINEAL
Crown Chakra

PITUITARY
Forehead
(3rd Eye)

THYROID
Throat Chakra

THYMUS
Heart Chakra

ADRENALS
Solar Plexus

LYDIG
Spleen Chakra

GONADS
Regenerative
Chakra

VIOLET
Spiritual

INDIGO
Intuition

BLUE
Inspiration

GREEN
Harmony &
Compassion

YELLOW
Intellect

ORANGE
Energy

RED
Life

# 7

## Within You Are All the Answers

### Techniques for Going Within

**Eternal Cosmos:** The blessings that each of you have are not yet fully understood. The fact is, your Subconscious Minds work with you, for you, and bring great good to you—if you but listen to the words of the Inner Selves as you become aware of who they are, what they are, and why they are with you.

Many of you are not yet fully understanding that you are instruments for a great and beautiful guidance from the Heightened Awareness and blessed actions of the Creator's Grace and from each one of your Teachers—your Super Consciousness, the High Self, the Subconscious Minds, the Master Teacher, the Doctor Teacher, and other Teachers and Guides. This guidance is the base upon which each of you builds your future and your knowledge that you will become bettered and increased as you listen and hear what they have to tell you.

Many of you do not take the time to listen. But we ask you to recognize that when you go outside to others—psychics, mediums, fortune tellers, and even the areas of therapy—you are not totally aware that *your* Teachers have guided you there, because you get the same information, but you are not aware that the Teachers are there. They send you to people who give you these words, repeating over and over again what your Subconscious, High Self, and all your Teachers and Guides try to have you understand is part of your plan.

Many of you do not realize how very great the Creative Source is in its Grace, and that each of you are loving, caring, and being loved and cared for in the beautiful, heightened awareness of your Higher Minds, which totally and completely give you wisdom, knowledge, and fulfillment—if you but listen!

Too many are so busy listening outside that they do not take the time to be quiet within and listen to what each one of these Teachers wants them to hear. *Please listen!* This is part of the plan, the teaching here—that you listen *within* as much as you do to those on the outer.

Sometimes you become involved with actions which are not part of your Karma, your timing, or your activity—you are simply trying to make things work for others *when your real task is to make things work for yourself!*

Please accept that this is the *greatest gift* you have been given in this lifetime. In each lifetime, the Subconscious brings someone to do this work, dealing with the Karma and Dharma patterns from the past to the present to the future that help, heal, and fulfill. Each of you, without knowing it, is fulfilling plans from many different lifetimes, so it becomes like a show, a theater, in which you have many characters standing on a stage working for your enjoyment, your appreciation, through comedy and drama.

Each of you has lived through, and is living through, comedy and drama. Each of you, understanding this, could make it better for yourselves if you recognize that when the play is over on the stage, you do not take home any of the dramas. You only remember that which made you laugh, that which made you understand certain situations from the actors on stage. *So see yourself as an actor or actress on stage working out the plan that the High Self and Subconscious Minds have arranged for you.*

You will find by looking at it like that, it is not something to overwhelm you, but to help you understand your Sacred Purpose—to give you the opportunity to fulfill that which is right action—not just for yourselves, but for that which is the memory bank in the Subconscious Awareness. The Subconscious Minds are always there for you! They will help you if you talk with them and ask them to give you the answers you seek from others.

Sometimes that which is verification comes from others, and it is rightful. But the main knowledge that comes from *within* is, many times, the only way you can fulfill the actions of your past, present, and future.

**Comment:** *Your discourse seems to have dealt with three of the Ten Steps in working with our Three Selves: Believing, Accepting, and Communicating with our Inner Selves and Teachers.*

**EC:** Correct. But the other steps are also important. If you take each step and carefully communicate with your Inner Selves about it, you will find that the steps are carefully handled by the Subconscious Minds to give you the full impact of what is rightful for their particular fulfillment, as well as your own. For you have come in to serve them, and they will give you all the accolades and help—if you accept that they are there to help you, not harm you.

Recognize that within each of you is a whole band of actors and actresses. If you will see it as a plan within a plan, that could make it easier for you to understand that you have come in to make the best of each lifetime. You have come in to fulfill it, not only with the Karma that has been given to you to handle and to fulfill, but for that which is your own particular desire to know, that you are on the planet Earth to help others understand and learn this particular truth that helps you and them to be fulfilled and fulfilling.

**Question:** *Would you recommend any techniques for hearing what is being said to people by their Subconscious?*

**EC:** At this point, each human being finds a different approach coming from their Inner Selves. Some people hear it in a voice. Some hear or see it in a dream. Some are, in every way, available to that which is a subconscious ability to bring balance and security to themselves, knowing they have come in to be of use, not only to themselves in helping them to fulfill their plan but also to be able to teach others.

Each of you has become a teacher in this work, whether you know that yet or not. You will be able to help people recognize what Luke meant when he said, "Physician, heal thyself." You will be able to do this through the three levels of Consciousness, through that within you that has brought all of these actions, problems—these challenges—and all of this activity, as well as joy and feeling good, within you when you listen to what is being taught.

*It is a schoolhouse filled with many Teachers and Guides who primarily ask you to talk to yourself.* When you were children and your mother or father did not listen to you, or your teachers did not hear you, you talked to Spirit or a friend who helped you. The same thing is true at this time. They are all your friends, wanting to help you to fulfill the plan.

Each one finds his own methods. But the major point is that within you are all the answers . . . once you have made contact in any way: dreams, hearing voices, or actually seeing things happen. Know that the blessed Creator loves each one of you and will give you what is rightful for you to fulfill your Sacred Purpose.

## Eternal Cosmos: Conclusion

Each of you has to know that within you are all the answers. You have to accept that's true. Sometimes one only needs verification by one's own Teachers and by knowledge that the Subconscious is guiding each one, fulfilling us from many past lives, not just a single past life. That is the beauty of these very great Inner Selves that help each of you. Talk to them. Communicate with them. It will help you fulfill the plan.

Each one has to listen to self as well as to others, for within the life plan, many times it is not easy to handle a Karmic Plan or be fulfilled, because sometimes a very difficult life plan makes what one does difficult to fulfill—to finish Karma or to bring in

Dharma to help someone else, *which is the major thrust this work teaches!*

Techniques are something each one learns from outside involvements, through meditation, contemplation, talking to teachers, psychics, sensitives, and others. But they always give you messages you have heard before—either from within or from someone else.

You are here to do the work for the Subconscious within you which brought you in, choosing parents that gave you the right to be strong by sometimes putting you out from home. Sometimes you think you are being harmed or hurt, but you are being given the right to be strong in your own image, to learn how to work with self, not just with someone else. Or not to be pampered, petted, and coddled so you depend on that instead of listening to that which says you have to be strong, *to do it yourself or it will never be accomplished. That is the key!*

# 8

## Meditation and Visualization
### to Fulfill the Subconscious Plan

**Eternal Cosmos:** The pattern of humans many times fails to recognize that certain teachings in different areas become part of changes in the lives of those who work with their own particular kind of understanding.

However, one of the greatest and most common actions, which at times people find difficult to accept, is *meditation*, which takes the Spirit out of the body and places it into various areas, leaving the body unlocked and empty—which of course becomes serious if the person is being attacked in any way.

We want to suggest another approach: *visualization*. Visualization could be fully involved with that which changes—brings balance, security, and fulfillment—to the human being. Visualization does this through the Subconscious Awareness, bringing about what one wishes to be, what one wishes to become, what one wishes to return to which is one's Sacred Purpose.

The reason we are suggesting visualization is that it is the same principle as meditation, except that you are totally aware that you are alive and well and looking at what you want from life—which is your Subconscious Minds very carefully planning the action so you become involved with that which they want.

Individuals can be sitting quietly and thinking carefully about what they want to be, what they want to do, what they know they can and will do—*and they can bring it about through visualizing it as being done.* In doing so, humans many times find that this type of action changes their lives to something much more balanced than if they turn themselves into a flying bird instead of resting, fulfilled, in an action that has feet on the ground yet its head in the sky.

Please remember that we only give suggestions in people's lives, for in many ways human beings become involved with what they are taught, what they are part of in their homes, their schools, or their churches. Sometimes this does not become what Teachers and Guides, in Spirit, recommend—unless the humans are willing to open their hearts and minds and look forward to that which gives them the opportunity to visualize whatever they wish from life within the pattern of their own particular activity. As Luke has said, "Physician, heal thyself." Visualization is one of the methods that can be used, definitely is used, and can handle many different kinds of changes for the better within the human world, the human actions and activities.

*Remember that each of you is a Creator*—a Creator of what is rightful and necessary to fulfill the plan that has brought you into the Light, into life, and into the Subconscious Awareness. Therefore, work with the Subconscious so it clearly brings you that which you visualize, what you wish from life, what you manifest from life, and what you make of that which is your life plan, your Sacred Purpose.

**Question:** *Is it true that external negative forces can sometimes take a person over and cause a life plan to go astray?*

**EC:** Yes. This means you must, within your own particular plan, pray before and after meditation or visualization to cleanse yourself of anything that is not yours, that you do not have to accept. If you do this successfully, you will find that the Subconscious will give you the plan in a way that makes its fulfillment possible, because that which has invaded is no longer present. The fulfillment of the plan of the Subconscious is to bring in that which finishes up old patterns and brings in new ones to fulfill them in the future, as well as the past and the present.

# 9

## An Explanation of Dedication

**Eternal Cosmos:** It is important for each one of you to recognize that you are part of something very important that is going on in the past, the present, and the future of the planet. The act of dedication to an important action or purpose can sometimes become so intense within humans that they forget that *the intensity of dedication can sometimes be wrong rather than right.*

For humans to dedicate themselves to something chosen, learned in school or church, or learned from parents, often has a way of challenging those humans to change their dedication in midstream to be part of that which is other than what their parents, churches, homes, or schools have said that they should be.

At times it is imperative that dedication then have a change of heart so it becomes dedication to what *your own* particular personal plan means to you, to fulfill your *Sacred Purpose* and to become fulfilled and fulfilling, not just for self, but for others you work for and with.

Dedication is good if you use it properly and do not push it to the wall, because dedication can become so intense that humans lose balance, lose whatever they are planning to do, because they have been told to do something that makes them dedicated to another person's cause rather than their own.

Please remember this, because in your particular causes up ahead you are going to find that you must listen to your own voice—your own voice within, your Subconscious Awareness—because you've come in to be dedicated to that which is *your right action.* Your Karma/Dharma has brought you in to fulfill some plan that many times is not what parents, or churches, or schools are teaching, but is that which you must learn from a totally new school, a totally new way of understanding self and what you are here to accomplish.

**Question: *If one has too much intensity, is there a tendency to bring in fear along with it?***

EC: Yes, but not just fear. Intensity can cause persons to be totally involved with what they are doing, or what they have been taught—*or what they are trying to manifest within that dedication which is truly not their own,* but someone else's teaching

Humans must learn to heal themselves. Learn to know that within you is your own particular voice, your own dedication to what you have come to do, for self as well as within the world. Make what you have come to do right, not just for those who taught you, but for that which you, in your own particular way, teach yourself.

Learn from yourself! Learn from your own particular understanding that dedication has a voice that must be heard—from self as well as others.

# 10

## Activating Your Purpose
### by Learning to Help Self
### in Order to Help Others

**Eternal Cosmos:** I want to note that each of you has been drawn into a group of this kind not for personal or subconscious reasons, but because each of you has come in at this time and this place to be of use to humanity.

You have also come in to keep your particular stability, your security, intact within your own life, as well as within your involvement with others who have entered into your life and into the life of each one who comes forward to fulfill your and their Sacred Purpose—to help, to heal, to supply humanity, not just self. Luke has said, "Physician, heal thyself," but that is within your personal need.

However, the world needs each one of you at this point—whether you recognize that or not. Some of you do go through certain kinds of Karmic memories,

125

but simply because in the past these memories were part of a change in time and place just as is happening now.

In other words, you are being challenged to remember, through your Subconscious, that you have been of use in the past much as you are being of use in the present. Some of you become so involved with self that you do not realize that in everything you learn, in everything that challenges you, you are able to help someone else overcome their particular misunderstanding of the reason they are in the world now.

Everyone who is part of prayer, part of groups, and part of actions—even the religious groups—no matter how intense they are, each one is on the planet at this time to make the world better.

Each one is here to bring the world into balance and security with the opportunity to heal or help—not for self alone but for those who are part of family, those who are involved with jobs and activities, who entertain, who bring in life and beauty and fulfillment through every action performed. Sometimes you may feel misunderstood or critical of yourself, or critical in feeling you are not accomplishing, when, in fact, you do not realize the situation is totally and completely correct.

Within your learning through these methods, you are able to help others who come to you with problems. You are able, in every way, to help them to understand that everything becomes fulfilled and fulfilling within periods of time when they complete an action of the past to benefit the present and the future.

If you understand this and activate your purpose in the area this is teaching you, you will be able to be much more secure within whatever is happening to you, because it becomes easier when you see that others have the same problems and do not know how to handle them. Because you are having that particular problem yourself, you are able to communicate and commune with these people to help them, because you are helping yourself at the same time.

Some have come to this Fellowship with hate and anger because they are not feeling wanted, needed, or loved. Yet that is the only way they could be strengthened, by moving through situations such as they go through but without being involved with that which coddles them or loves them or makes them feel someone else must help them. That help must be strengthened and secured within themselves. This is, invariably, something which is learned over periods of time.

The human being recognizes that sometimes parents who do not love, parents who do not coddle, parents who do not pay attention, simply are giving the opportunity to the human child to learn, to stand on its own two feet, to be involved with its own stability and security, so the child can teach someone else the same lesson it has learned through this lack of what it feels was caring or love from parents, or family, or jobs, or whatever the child is involved with that seems to be destructive rather than strengthening.

When these humans look back after a certain length of time, they can see that in every way they have learned lessons through these lacks that make them more able to help someone else who has the same lacks, and therefore they have become better human beings, healers, and helpers in ways that often are beyond their comprehension.

*Do understand that each one of you has chosen this,* has chosen to be an instrument to help others become fulfilled and fulfilling through that which they learned, through that which they have become involved with through stress and, many times, actions that make them unhappy, until they recognize they are being strengthened, secured, and— indeed very often—fulfilled.

At times, it is difficult to accept that you, according to your own feelings, are suffering in vain. Suffering, however, sometimes is that which humans find makes them stronger in many ways. Suffering and pain in general may become so intense that when the pain disappears through someone else's helping, through someone else bringing a cure, the release from the suffering and pain becomes so satisfying that those released from it are able then to help others who have pain.

Do recognize that you are healers and helpers, and you are in every way learning the lessons that give you the right to be healers and helpers, and that you have come in purposely to be that which you have turned out to be, whether you know it or not.

As we have been saying over and over again— *prayer works*! Everyone who has troubles, prays—in some way or another, sometimes angrily, sometimes with great stress. But as long as it is not done with hate or anger or that which opens psychic doors—the Chakras—to that which is negative-evil, each one learns lessons through pain and the ability to be able to stand it until it disappears.

**Question:** *Would you say the purpose of the Fellowship's work is to help individuals activate their purpose?*

**EC:** Exactly. Activating your purpose does not really mean *your* purpose. *Your* purpose is what you accepted from the Subconscious Awareness, and if you talk to your Subconscious—and your High Self as well, through the Subconscious—you will find that many answers will come, which will make it easier to handle a situation or handle other people's situations because you have learned how to do so.

It is like a schoolhouse you are constantly in. The school has good teachers. Sometimes the teachers in the school become determined to make you listen to what they have to teach. Sometimes it is difficult when a child does not feel what is being taught is fair, or that movement is taking place by way of someone else's dictates. But you will see that when you learn the lessons, no matter where they come from, you are freed of the past and are able to perform actions that help others to be freed also.

**Comment:** *One problem of mine in this lifetime was the most difficult I ever had. I spent thirteen years consciously working at it. It was forgiving someone—forgiving a person. One particular person.*

**EC:** You were involved for thirteen years with a past-life pattern in which, perhaps, you were the very image of the person you were trying to forgive, or of others who could not and did not understand and caused you pain and suffering. In other words, *you were seeing your reflection in that person.* And because you did handle it, did work with it, you received a gift of something so beautiful that the fulfillment was then rightful, because you no longer had to look back.

You had a partner who gave you everything you truly needed, and you worked it out by staying with the situation until it was completed. Something was always given to you, even though at the time it seemed not rightful.

We want you to think about what was said here, because many people suffer from a lack of financial security and a lack of many different kinds of loving care, because within them *they expect things to be what they want them to be*, and it never is quite that way until the action is complete.

Sometimes human beings expect more from their companions, from those they work with and for. It becomes very overwhelming *when they realize they are not going to get that fulfillment until they learn to understand they must give in order to receive*. And that is the key!

Forgiveness is one of the greatest gifts humans can have: forgiving that which is no longer rightful, to have compassion for self and others in actions that seem to be hurtful but actually are challenging. Remember, the challenge can be worked with, and for, to become fulfilling. If you do not accept that challenge, you simply go on and on and become totally involved with something which makes it worse, not better.

**Q:** *EC, some time ago I attended a church and was given a meditation method on forgiveness which was very, very healing for me. It is a wonderful method, very simple and very loving. Is that something you feel is needed at this time?*

**EC:** Religion is meant to help humans, to bring them into a full realization that they have come to be part of a group action to help others as well as self, and most religious groups use prayer and use forgiveness. Any method that gives you a feeling of accomplishment has value. Where it comes from doesn't matter as long as it is used correctly and fulfills self.

**Comment:** *I often think I could help other people with this same method.*

**EC:** Of course you can! That is why you learned it. It has no beginning and no end. It is what you learned to help self, so you could help others. That is the whole method—to learn it and then use what you have been given to help others.

That is your purpose! And you definitely do that within the beauty of the teachings you are involved with. Every teaching you have ever gotten has been to help someone else, not just self. And that is what you have come to do.

Let me bless each one of you for being part of this very interesting way of learning lessons, whether they seem they are going to be instructive or not.

*Each lesson, just as in school, becomes a fulfill-
ment of purpose.* If you activate it within your own
particular love and understanding, you can help
many other people through what you have learned.
Sometimes you have learned it through pain and
stress, but always within an action in which you
know the end result is something of good—not that
which is harmful but that which is helpful. Remember that!

# 11

## Counting Your Blessings

### An Explanation of the Fellowship's System of Numerology from Spirit

*William Miller, D.D.*

One intriguing feature of the Three Selves work of the Fellowship of Universal Guidance is its description of the important role that *numbers* and *numerology* play in our lives.

Numerology is based on the universal vibrational energies of numbers and what those energies represent. It is thought to have originated in the ancient mystery schools, of which perhaps the most famous was the School of Pythagoras, the Greek philosopher and mathematician, who was born around 582 B.C.

Numbers affect us on all levels, especially our subconscious memory patterns of Karma (unfinished business from the past; what we failed to complete) and Dharma (the talents, skills, and gifts of Spirit we earned from past-life service and completion and are now able to use to help others overcome their Karma). The Fellowship's system of numerology takes into consideration the Karmic/Dharmic memory patterns that the Subconscious Minds—through their instrument, the human Consciousness—use to fulfill the Life Plan, with the help of the High Self. Various numerology texts and other sources may give meanings for numbers that are different from the meanings used at the Fellowship. Those other meanings are no less valid than ours; they simply pertain to aspects of life that are different from what the Fellowship's unique approach deals with.

Each of us has a Birth *Path* number and a Birth *Year* number within a nine-year cycle. The Birth *Path* number is derived by adding together the month, day, and year numbers of *the date we were actually born*, until the result is a single number between 1 and 9. The Birth *Year* number is derived by adding together the same numbers in the same fashion, except we substitute the *current* year number for the birth-year number.

For example, the Birth *Path* number for someone born on 3-23-1954 (i.e., 3+5+1) is 9. In 2005, the Birth *Year* number for that person is based on 3-23-2005 (i.e., 3+5+7) and thus is 6.

From birth to maturity and to transition, we are influenced materially and spiritually by our numbers during each year of our lives. Within right timing, which is determined by our Subconscious as well as our High Self's awareness of our Karmic/Dharmic plan, the numbers affect our completion of our *Sacred Purpose*, our contract with our Subconscious and High Self.

We always have Free Will, and our Subconscious and Conscious Minds can accept or reject whatever opportunities and/or challenges are presented during a nine-year cycle. Numbers, like the planets in astrology, *impel* our lives but do not *compel* us to do anything against our will. Thus, numerology is a *tool*—for heightening Consciousness, for spiritual fulfillment, and for material success.

## A Description of the Nine Birth-Year Numbers

Each of the years in a nine-year cycle has a particular energy, which can be described as follows:

**#1 Year**: Represents New Beginnings—new choices and new understandings, with the commencement of a nine-year cycle.

**#2 Year**: Can represent Strength and Courage when the numbers added together equal 20 (= 2). But can also represent an Escape or "Run-away" number when the numbers added together equal 11 (= 2).

For example, a birth date of 9-16-1912 equals 9+7+4 = 20, or 2 (Strength and Courage). But 2 can also represent an Escape or "Run-away" pattern, as explained above. The word "escape" is often mistranslated. It does not necessarily mean leaving life. It can mean leaving an old pattern for something new. It can also be a challenge not to quit a pattern that has, over and over again, been brought forth Karmically for completion—for example, a marriage in which one partner has abandoned the other in many lifetimes and has returned this lifetime to bring the marriage finally into fulfillment.

**#3 Year**: Involved with Constant Change (work, life plan, etc.).

**#4 Year**: A platform for Material Security. It is a practical year of "grounding" oneself in the material world; also it is a platform for the Spiritual Temple coming forth in Year 5.

**#5 Year**: The Material-World Platform, with the addition of the Creator's essence of Heightened Awareness (God blended with the human).

**#6 Year**: ("3 + 3") The first "3" represents heightened Spiritual Awareness. The second "3" represents Material Security. Both work together to bring balance to the human.

**#7 Year**: Spiritual Strength, Courage, and Determination to fulfill one's plan.

**#8 Year**: The beautiful number 8 represents the Energy of the Creator flowing down into the human and back to God: God and the human blended.

**#9 Year**: The year of Fulfillment and Evolvement for the greatest good of the Karmic/Dharmic pattern. This is the completion of the nine-year cycle.

## Rebirth Years & Womb Years

Two of the years that represent the greatest challenge are the Rebirth Years and the Womb Years.

**Rebirth Year.** When the Birth Path number and Birth Year number are the *same*—for example, 3-23-1954 (= 3+5+1 = 9) and 3-23-1999 (= 3+5+1 = 9)—that indicates a year of *Rebirth*. It is a time when one is in the image, figuratively not literally, of being a baby.

A baby needs to be held, coddled, and loved. This is usually not a time to initiate major new projects or life-changes. It is a time to have fun and enjoy life. Often, memory patterns from childhood recur— especially as physical challenges to the body, if one has a history of childhood or genetic ailments.

**Womb Year.** A Womb Year is a year that's one year *prior* to a Rebirth Year. In the above example, a person with an actual birthday of 3-23-1954 (Birth Path = 9) would have a Rebirth Year every time the Birth Year also = 9 (i.e., 1963, 1972, 1981, 1990,

1999, 2008, etc.). For that person, the Womb Years, being one year earlier than the Rebirth Years, would be 1962, 1971, 1980, 1989, 1998, 2007, etc., (i.e., whenever the Birth Year = 8). Figuratively, being in a Womb Year is comparable to a child in the womb preparing for birth (or in this case, rebirth), and it is time to "go with the flow" and not push or jam actions on any level. In the womb, the baby can kick and scream but not avoid birth/rebirth unless it wishes to abort itself.

Again, numerology is one of many tools we can use to heighten our Consciousness, and it is a core part of the Fellowship's Counseling and Three Selves work. Numbers help explain how our past, present, and future are tied into our Karma and Dharma as our Life plan, our Sacred Purpose, is fulfilled. We may also use numerology to understand others: our parents, mates, children, employers, and others in our lives.

There are many mysteries to be understood, and numerology helps us unravel some of them, guiding us in our daily lives as we remember that prayer, Light, and rapport with our Inner Selves and High Self, all blessed by the Creator's Grace, can navigate us to that which is for the Highest Good of all concerned within God's Will.

# Mantra Prayer of Protection

Father Mother—GOD,
I ask that I be cleared and cleansed
Within the Universal White Christ* Light,
The Green Healing Light,
And the Purple Transmuting Flame.

Within GOD's Will
And for my highest good,
I ask that any and all
Negative evil energies
Be completely sealed in their own Light,
Encapsulated within the Ultraviolet Light,
Cut off and removed from me.

Impersonally,
With neither love nor hate,
I return all negative evil energies
To their source of emanation,
Decreeing that they never again
Be allowed to reestablish themselves
Within me or anyone else in any form.**

I now ask that I be placed
Within a triple electromagnetic shield
Of the Universal White Christ* Light of Protection
And for this Blessing, I give thanks.

Amen

---

\* *The word "Christ" is optional. "Christ" is an energy of the Universal White Light of the Creator—not a man. Many great teachers, such as Jesus, Krishna, Moses, Buddha, Mohammed, etc., were Christed beings.*

\*\* *What you don't want or need, you don't have to accept.*

Other publications from
The Fellowship of Universal Guidance:
*Pathways to Your Three Selves*


Services offered by
The Fellowship of Universal Guidance include:

- Prayers for individuals and for our planet
- Wisdom publications
- Classes for individual and collective growth
- Membership in our Fellowship family

For further information and a virtual tour,
please visit our Web site at
www.foug.org


Or contact:
**Fellowship of Universal Guidance, Inc.**
1524 W. Glenoaks Blvd.
Glendale, CA 91201
Telephone: (818) 500–9445 · Fax: (818) 500–8235